1993

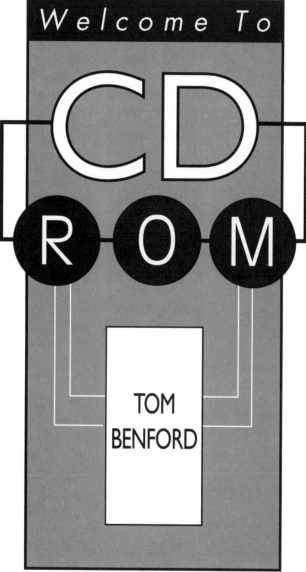

Welcome To

CD
ROM

TOM
BENFORD

MIS:
PRESS

A Subsidiary of
Henry Holt and Co., Inc.

First Edition—1993

ISBN 1-55828-265-3

Printed in the United States of America.

10 9 8 7 6 5 4 3 2 1

MIS:Press books are available at special discounts for bulk purchases for sales promotions, premiums, fund-raising, or educational use. Special editions or book excerpts can also be created to specification.

For details contact: Special Sales Director
MIS:Press
a subsidiary of Henry Holt and Company, Inc.
115 West 18th Street
New York, New York 10011

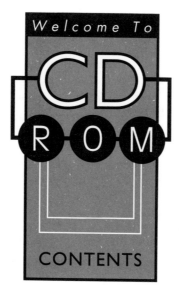

Welcome To

CD ROM

CONTENTS

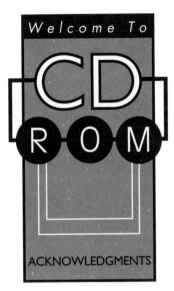

Welcome To
CD
ROM
ACKNOWLEDGMENTS

I'd like to thank the following individuals and companies for the invaluable help, cooperation, and assistance they provided me in preparing this book. My thanks and appreciation go to: John Wagner at NEC's Optical Media Division; Glenn Ochsenreiter, Director of the MPC Marketing Council; the Software Publishers Association *CD-ROM SIG*; Larry Boden, General Manager of Nimbus Information Systems; Chris Andrews, President of UniDisc; Patrick Diggins at QB Products; Mary Vaughn and Patrice Silarski at Metatec/Discovery Systems; Jack and George at Dover 1-Hour Photo; Pete Clark, Scott Megill and Jon Squire for their editorial research assistance; Dennis Burke at Quanta Press; Helene Dashefsky at Educorp/Gazelle Technologies; Chandran Cheriyan at Apple Computer; Larry O'Shaughnessy at Eastman Kodak; Fran McGeehee and Tony Magoulas at Tandy Corporation; Tim and Marilyn Benford for their encouragement and support; Cary Sullivan, my development editor and Joanne Kelman, my production editor at MIS:Press; and Heide Lange, my literary agent at Sanford J. Greenburger Associates, for her enthusiasm, support and hard work. I'm especially grateful to Liz Benford for her photography, organization, followup, moral support, and the incredible amount of patience and good humor she exhibited during this entire project. Thanks also to all the individuals, public relations firms, and manufacturers too numerous to mention individually, who also aided me in various capacities to make this book possible.

Tom Benford
February 1, 1993

*For my wife and life partner, Liz, who shared my vision
and encouraged me to pursue it—I love you.*

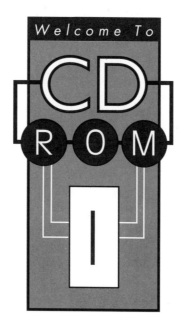

INTRODUCTION TO CD-ROM

In this lesson...

…What CD-ROM is

…How CD-ROM compares to magnetic computer media

…CD-ROM and its impact on information storage & exchange

…An overview of the binary system, ASCII codes and data storage

…Some commonly-used CD-ROM terms

Welcome to the world of CD-ROM, an exciting new dimension of personal computing.

CD-ROM is the most innovative advance in publishing since Johann Gutenberg invented movable type in 1447. CD-ROM has been called "the new papyrus" because, like the invention of paper, it is a revolutionary means of storing, retrieving and disseminating huge amounts of information.

CD-ROM is an acronym that stands for Compact Disc Read-Only Memory. CD-ROM is an optical data storage medium for computers that uses laser light to read the binary information it contains.

To give you some examples of how much information a CD-ROM can hold, consider this: a 5 inch CD-ROM disc stores more than .7 gigabyte of data (716,800,000 bytes or "characters"). That's more than 1,900 floppy disks or in excess of over 250,000 typewritten pages. The entire contents of large works such as the Bible (complete Old and New Testaments) fit on a CD-ROM with plenty of room to spare.

But that's not all. In addition to text matter, CD-ROM can also contain audio (sound) and visual (graphic) information. So words, pictures, illustrations, sound, music, and even moving images can be stored in binary format on a CD-ROM disc for retrieval and use with a personal computer. To give you some additional examples of CD-ROM capacity, consider that over 74 minutes of audio or over 5,000 high-resolution, full-color images can easily fit on a disc.

CD-ROM makes it possible to have a wealth of information literally at your fingertips. Never before has it been possible to provide so much data to so many people at such a low cost.

Humanity has reached a new plateau in technology. For the first time in history more information is available electronically on computers than it is on paper. For thousands of years paper has been the medium and repository of permanent information. In today's world paper is now merely a transient hard-copy proofing device that can be disposed of and recycled, since the data itself exists in binary data format. This fact certainly makes CD-ROM one of the most important tools of this century, and one of the landmark technological developments of all time. CD-

ROM's importance and acceptance will continue to grow as the need to store, access, and distribute information continues to increase.

OPTICAL MEDIA refers to CD-ROM or any other medium (such as laserdisc) that utilizes light, lenses, mirrors, or other optical components for the storage and retrieval of data.

DEFINITION

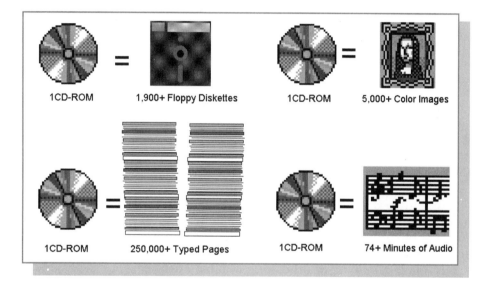

1CD-ROM	1,900+ Floppy Diskettes
1CD-ROM	5,000+ Color Images
1CD-ROM	250,000+ Typed Pages
1CD-ROM	74+ Minutes of Audio

FIGURE 1.1 CD-ROM has tremendous storage capacity. A single CD-ROM disc holds more data than 1,900 floppy diskettes, or over 250,000 typewritten pages, or in excess of 5,000 high-resolution color images, or over 74 minutes of audio.

CD-ROM is referred to as *optical media,* since light (from a laser) and lenses (optics) are used to read the data encoded on the discs. This is one of the major differences between CD-ROM and *magnetic media* (the floppy and hard disks you normally use with your computer), which rely on magnetism to write and read data.

The term CD-ROM stands for compact disc read-only memory, and that describes precisely what CD-ROM is and what it does: it's a compact disc that "remembers" data that only can be read from it. The CD-ROM discs used by computers are virtually identical to the audio CDs you listen to on your stereo at home, but computer CD-ROMs can also contain text and graphics in addition to sound.

Like audio CD's, computer CD-ROMs allow data to be read from them but they do not allow altering (editing) that data or adding (writing) to it. Hence the name "read-only memory" is accurate, since you can read from it but you can't write to it as you can with magnetic media, such as floppy or hard disks.

To extend the point further, in the purest sense even audio CDs can correctly be called CD-ROM since you can't "write" to them either. However, to avoid confusion let's refer to the music CDs you listen to simply as audio CDs to make the distinction between them and the computer CD-ROMs.

BINARY DATA FORMAT

Data is stored on CD-ROMs in *binary format*, which is the native language of personal computers. The binary coding system uses only two characters to convey data: the one (1) and the zero (0). This two-conditional format can also represent a "true" (1) or a "false" (0) condition, or an "on" (1) or "off" (0) signal to a computer circuit. By combining the ones and zeroes in different orders it is possible to represent every character, letter, number, symbol, or other data in binary format.

Computers are especially good at handling simple bits of information, like 1/0, yes/no, on/off, odd/even and so forth, so all data and instructions are reduced to this simple form for processing by the PC.

It might help to think of binary coding as being similar to the dots and dashes of Morse code (even though binary and Morse code are quite different, the overall principal of a two-character system is basically the same and it makes understanding the concept easier).

In the binary system, each column to the left doubles the value of the column to its immediate right. By contrast, in the decimal system each column to the left is ten times the value of the column to its immediate right. In decimal, working from right to left, the column designations are ones, tens, hundreds, thousands, hundred thousands, millions, and so forth. In binary, also going from right to left, the columns are 1, 2, 4, 8,

TABLE 1.1 *Binary code consists of combinations of ones and zeroes to represent all kinds of data. Binary is the native language of computers.*

DECIMAL NUMBER	SAME NUMBER IN BINARY
0	00000000
1	00000001
2	00000010
3	00000011
4	00000100
5	00000101
6	00000110
7	00000111
8	00001000
9	00001001

16, 32, 64, 128, and so forth. In the decimal system, any column can have a value of 0-9. In binary, any column can only be 1 or 0.

Since only values of zero or one are valid to a computer, all of its processing is based on these two digits. This is why personal computers are called *digital* devices.

DIGITAL means related to digits or the way they are represented. For all practical purposes here, digital is synonymous with binary because personal computers store and process information coded as combinations of binary digits (bits).

Microscopic wells called *pits* are contained on the CD-ROMs surface, and these pits are the equivalent of ones in binary (or dots in Morse code). The flat surfaces between these pits are called *lands* and they represent the zeroes in binary (or dashes in Morse code). A more detailed and illustrated account of how CD-ROMs store and read data is contained in Appendix C. The important thing to remember here is that CD-ROMs store all data (photographs, drawings, words, sounds, pictures, computer commands, and so forth) in binary format.

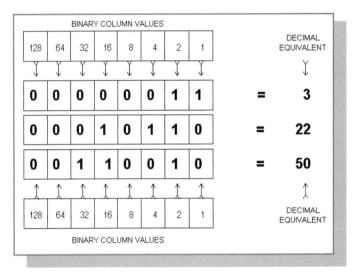

FIGURE 1.2 *The placement of the ones determines the value of a binary number. As each column place moves to the left it doubles in value each time.*

A computer character (such as a letter, number, or punctuation mark) is represented in binary format as a byte. A byte is made up of 8 bits (either ones or zeroes).

A **BYTE** is a unit of information used in computer processing and storage consisting of 8 bits which, by their order, represent a single character.

The numerical (binary) value of each byte represents a corresponding ASCII code. ASCII, an abbreviation for American Standard Code for Information Interchange, is an internationally accepted character coding system used for the exchange of information between computers. ASCII provides 256 values that are used to represent letters, numerals, punctuation, printer and communication control codes, and graphic and special characters.

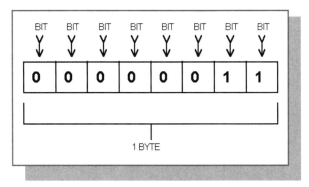

FIGURE 1.3 *A byte represents one character of data and is composed of eight bits (binary digits).*

ASCII (pronounced ask-ee), an acronym for the American Standard Code for Information Interchange, is an internationally accepted coding scheme that assigns numeric values to letters, numbers, punctuation marks, and control characters to enable computers to communicate with each other.

The first half (codes 0 through 127) comprise the *standard set*; these codes use 7 active bits and contain communication and printer control codes as well as the capital and lower-case alpha/numeric characters and punctuation marks. The second half, known as the *extended set* (codes 128 through 255), uses 8 active bits and contains the graphic and special characters.

MAGNETIC MEDIA VS. OPTICAL MEDIA

CD-ROM has some things in common with magnetic media, but there are also some major differences between the two as well. Being aware of the similarities as well as the differences will aid you in understanding and getting the most from CD-ROM right from the start.

First, let's take a look at the proper spelling of the two media. Floppy and hard disks are always spelled with a "k" ending for the word "disk" (or diskette) when referring to magnetic media. Conversely, "disc" with a "c" refers to CD-ROM or audio compact discs. The different spellings provide a subtle yet easy means of distinguishing between which is which.

Floppy diskettes, whether they are the 5.25 inch or 3.5 inch size, are called *removable media* since they can be removed from the computer's floppy disk drive and used on other machines. They normally can't hold too much data, however (1.44 megabytes, or about 1.5 million bytes or characters is the maximum). Floppy disks are very inexpensive, and are the principal way of distributing software. Floppies (once they are formatted) are easy and ready to use as soon as they are inserted into the disk drive.

The computer's hard drive is called *non-removable* or *fixed media* since the magnetic media itself is permanently mounted inside the hard disk drive unit. Hard drives can typically hold from 20 to several hundred megabytes, depending on the capacity. Hard drives are expensive, costing hundreds to thousands of dollars.

CD-ROM brings the best features of floppy and hard disks together. CD-ROM provides as much data storage capacity as the largest, most expensive hard drives. CD-ROM is removable, relatively inexpensive, and easy to use, like floppy diskettes.

CD-ROM is fast becoming a popular means of publishing and distributing computer software, especially as programs and databases get larger and more complex.

MAGNETIC MEDIA refers to floppy diskettes, hard disks, and tape backup units or other devices that use magnetism (rather than light and optics) to write and read data.

The floppy disks and the hard drive in your PC are magnetic media since they rely on magnetism for recording and reading data. The surface of the media (the brown-colored disk itself inside the square black envelope) is coated with a very fine layer of magnetic particles used to record data. The magnetic write heads on the disk drive use electromagnetism to arrange these particles into patterns which represent the data. The drive can also read these patterns (of data) by scanning these magnetic particles on the disk surface.

The ability to write (save) data to a magnetic disk makes file management and computing as we know it possible, so magnetic media is indispensable for all practical purposes. Magnetic media can be thought of as semi-permanent data storage, since any data contained on it can be changed or removed. For the majority of our temporary day-to-day data storage purposes it also provides a convenient and reasonably inexpensive solution. Unlike CD-ROMs, which can't be erased, magnetic media can be reused by simply recording new information over the old. In essence, the new material is written over the old.

While the capability of writing and editing data on magnetic media is certainly convenient, the danger of accidentally erasing important information is also ever-present. And even though floppy disks can be protected from accidental erasure by covering their write-protect notch, their data can also be rendered unusable by dust, dirt, a fingerprint, smudge, or other foreign material on the disk's magnetic surface. Even a relatively weak magnetic field, like that of a small refrigerator magnet or even a magnetic screwdriver blade, can destroy the data on a disk, another disadvantage of magnetic media. And because there is physical contact between the read/write heads and the disk surface, eventually the disk wears out and becomes unreliable for storing data.

Data on a CD-ROM is read using laser light, a lens and other components instead of magnetism, so there is no physical contact between the CD-ROM and the reader. Only a beam of light touches the data encoded on the CD-ROM. CD-ROMs are impervious to magnetism and, while not indestructible, provide a highly-stable medium for storing data. With reasonable care CD-ROMs should last for many years or even decades. But don't forget that the ROM portion of CD-ROM stands for read-only memory, so data on the CD-ROM can't be changed, added to, or erased.

It's not a competition or matter of choosing which is better. Both magnetic and optical media have their own specific features and uses, and there is a place for them both in the personal computing environment.

As we learned earlier, CD-ROM has tremendous storage capacity, which makes it an ideal medium for holding large volumes of information. Entire encyclopedias, dictionaries, literary classics, clip-art libraries, and more are all available on CD-ROM, ready for instant access whenever you need them.

Convenience and portability are other advantages of CD-ROM. With a diameter of about 5 inches, CD-ROMs are the same physical size as audio CDs, so they're easy to store and transport. In fact, the same storage racks and cabinets used for audio CDs can serve double-duty for CD-ROM discs as well.

In addition to increasing your productivity by putting a world of information literally at your fingertips, CD-ROM also expands the capabilities of your PC as well. With a CD-ROM drive installed, you'll be able to play your favorite audio CDs as well as CD-ROM discs while you continue your other computing tasks. And, with the proper software, you'll be able to take advantage of multimedia that combines sights, sounds and text data—even full-motion video playback is possible with CD-ROM.

While CD-ROM is new and exciting, you'll be amazed at how quickly you will come to regard it as an essential part of your computing sessions. To give you a practical example, I used CD-ROM several times while writing this chapter to find out what year Gutenberg invented movable type, to get a listing of the ASCII code, and to confirm my definitions of several terms.

It's been said that the longest journey begins with but a single step. Your journey into the exciting and information-filled world of CD-ROM is already well underway!

REVIEW...

CD-ROM...

...has tremendous storage capacity.

...is revolutionizing the way large amounts of information are stored and distributed.

...is optical media containing binary code.

...uses laser light, lenses, and optics.

...is a read-only medium.

...is as easy to use as a floppy diskette.

…is more permanent that magnetic media.

…looks and feels like an audio compact disc.

…can contain text, pictures, and sound all at the same time.

…makes huge amounts of data easily accessible.

…is an inexpensive, stable, portable, and removable data-storage medium.

…uses a "c" in the spelling of compact disc to distinguish it from magnetic disk.

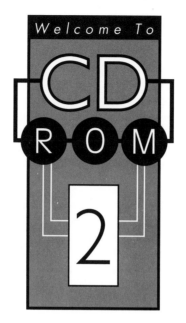

Welcome To

CD ROM

2

WHAT CD-ROM CAN DO FOR YOU

In this lesson...

…What makes CD-ROM a superior reference resource

…Some points about CD-ROM data retrieval

…Business applications

…Educational applications

…Recreational applications

…Special interest databases

...Governmental, library and institutional uses

...Limited edition/internal-use CD-ROMs

...More terms and definitions

Virtually any material that can be (or ever has been) published can be encoded on CD-ROM and, subsequently, become endowed with superior accessibility far beyond what is possible on paper, microfiche, or any other medium. Data on CD-ROM can be processed by the personal computer making it all instantly available.

MICROFICHE is a non-computerized storage medium that uses a sheet of photographic film to record highly-reduced images of entire pages of data too small to be read with the naked eye. A projection machine, called a microfiche reader, enlarges the microfiche images for reading or reference.

Information on CD-ROM is more dynamic because it can be searched, cross-referenced, linked, copied, and used in innumerable ways, depending on the disc's contents and your needs. Harnessing the power of the personal computer and linking it to the incredible storage capabilities of CD-ROM has made it possible for us all to be active participants in the Information Age. Never before in history has man had such an abundance of knowledge and accumulated data available and such a powerful means of accessing it. This is truly a wondrous and exciting time to be alive.

INFORMATION AGE is a term used in Alvin Toffler's book, *The Third Wave*, that refers to the phase of societal development we have recently entered. The Information Age was ushered-in by the advent of satellites, personal computers, fax machines, cellular phones, and increased communication efficiency. Information, and the ability to exchange and deploy it instantaneously, is the most important commodity of the Information Age, replacing agriculture and manufacturing as the mainstay industries of the economy.

DATA RETRIEVAL

Since CD-ROMs hold collections of data, they can rightly be called databases. More often than not, the amount of data contained in a typical CD-ROM application can involve tens or even hundreds of thousands of individual records. A means of finding and retrieving specific information is, therefore, an essential component.

DATABASE means any aggregate collection of data. Relating to computers and CD-ROM, a database is a file or files composed of individual records for each entry in a file. Each record is composed of separate fields that can be used for searching, sorting, or separating specific information.

Retrieval Software

Virtually every CD-ROM comes with its own retrieval software supplied either on the CD-ROM itself or on an accompanying floppy disk. The retrieval software, as its name implies, is used to setup the required environment for retrieving the CD-ROM data with your particular computer system. Typically, the retrieval software prompts you for particular information it needs to do its jobs, such as what drive letter is assigned for the CD-ROM drive and where you wish to store any information copied from the CD-ROM (floppy disk, hard disk, a specific file name or subdirectory, and so on).

While the retrieval software varies from one CD-ROM to another, generally speaking it is always straight-forward and easy to use. What form the retrieval software takes depends to a large degree on the type of information the CD-ROM contains. For example, a disc containing clip-art or photographic images might only contain a text file providing a listing of the contents or categories and a viewing utility for getting a look at the image files. A CD-ROM containing text-based information (like the Bible, for example) might not provide any content listing but provide a powerful means for searching the entire content of the disc to find a particular word, name, phrase, or other desired target. Application-specific CD-ROMs, like games or demonstration discs, may have been designed to retrieve specific information only and execute a predetermined program, giving the user few (if any) options in using the software.

Some CD-ROMs provide a listing file that can either be viewed on the computer monitor or printed out using a line printer for easy reference. The listing generally contains information about the specific files contained on the CD-ROM, along with a description of the file contents, what commands, keystrokes, or mouse movements are required to access the file, and where it is located on the CD-ROM.

DOS-BASED refers to any application or utility that operates directly from the MS-DOS operating system rather than through an alternate environment or operating system, such as Windows or OS/2.

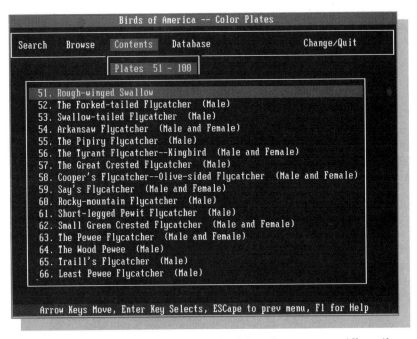

FIGURE 2.1 This is a good example of drop-down menus. All available selection categories and subcategories are presented as menu items that can be selected either through the keyboard or by pointing and clicking with a mouse.

Very often a drop-down menu interface is used that makes using the retrieval software literally a point-and-click operation. This type of interface has become increasingly popular for DOS-based retrieval, whereas retrieval software running under Windows and OS/2 is already based on the Graphical User Interface or GUI.

GUI (pronounced gooey) is an acronym for Graphical User Interface. GUIs use icons, drop-down menus, or other visual representations to initiate computer commands, run programs, exchange files, and perform other tasks using a mouse or keyboard rather than typed commands. GUIs are more intuitive and easier to use than entering commands directly at the system command prompt. The Apple Macintosh, Microsoft Windows, and IBM's OS/2 are all examples of GUIs.

FIGURE 2.2 A GUI uses icons rather than words or typed commands, as shown in the example above. Clicking on any of the icon boxes below the picture with a mouse activates the function it represents.

Searching

Locating a particular piece of information is usually only a matter of specifying a unique series of characters (called a *string*) contained in the target data so the computer knows what you're looking for. Boolean operators are usually supported to further refine the search and zero-in on that which you seek.

DEFINITION

BOOLEAN OPERATORS, also known as logical operators, are based upon Boolean algebra and are conditional parameters that check for logical conjunctions (AND), logical inclusions (OR), an exclusive "or" condition (XOR), and logical exclusions (NOT). Databases usually rely on these Boolean operators to qualify the target data during text searches.

The ability to combine search criteria by using Boolean operators greatly increases the speed and accuracy of locating the specific information you want. For example, let's say you're using a CD-ROM database that contains the fax telephone numbers of over a half-million businesses nationwide. You need the fax number of a company called ACME Electrical Components (or ACME Electronic Parts or ACME Electro, or something like that). All you know for sure is that the company's name begins with ACME, so you type in "Acme" at the search prompt. Within a few seconds a listing of over two hundred companies with Acme beginning their names appears on the screen. Then you remember the company is located somewhere in New Jersey, so you start another search, but this time you specify "Acme" at the search prompt along with the Boolean operator "and" and specify "NJ" as the second qualifier. The retrieval software finds Acme Electronic Components in Edison, New Jersey within seconds and you have the company's complete mailing address along with the fax phone number you needed. The Boolean operator made the computer search skip over every Acme that did not meet the second search criterion (NJ).

AVAILABLE NOW...ON CD-ROM

As you've already learned, a single CD-ROM can hold volumes of information and effective retrieval software makes all of the data contained on a disc immediately accessible. That's why CD-ROM is such a superior ready-reference resource. Let's take a look at how CD-ROM is being used in several different areas.

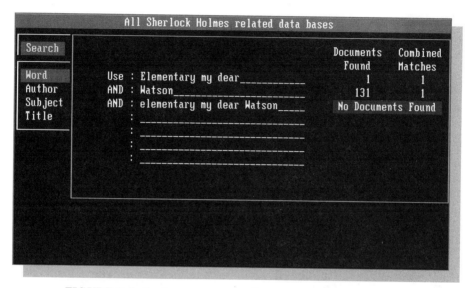

FIGURE 2.3 *Boolean operators allow combining target words or phrases to make finding specific data fast and easy. The example above shows "hits" for the first two targets but none for the third.*

Practical Applications

Business uses for CD-ROM are as numerous and varied as are the types of businesses in operation. Standard reference works including dictionaries and encyclopedias are available on CD-ROM, and these discs often contain other information such as an atlas and population/economic information that may be useful to the business user as well. Clip-art collections abound on CD-ROM, making thousands of professionally-drawn images instantly available for use in desktop publishing, art, or design work.

Stock photography collections are also available on CD-ROM that provide instant access to high-quality color and black-and-white photo libraries. Typeface libraries containing thousands of fonts ready for downloading are also available for desktop publishing or other graphic arts applications. Economic, geographic, import/export, agricultural and manufacturing data, and more is all available on CD-ROM for the business user, as are nationwide business telephone and fax listings, to cite but a few business uses for CD-ROM.

Education

Educational uses for CD-ROM abound. There are discs for preschoolers that teach colors and shape identification, basic concepts (like up/down or in-out), the alphabet and much more. And, since CD-ROM is used with a computer, the youngster also learns basic computing skills like pointing and clicking a mouse in the process of using the discs.

Numerous great literary works are available on CD-ROM for the student (the complete collection of *Monarch Notes* is also available on CD-ROM for those who like short-cuts). Specific compendium titles are available on CD-ROM that include the entire lifework of specific authors. For example, if you're a Sherlock Holmes fan you can get a CD-ROM with Arthur Conan Doyle's entire collection of stories and articles, along with the original woodcut illustrations that appeared in the *Saturday Evening Post*. Shakespearean students and enthusiasts can get all of Will's works collected on a single CD-ROM. Encyclopedias, dictionaries, thesauruses, grammar and style books, and many other literary reference works are available from several vendors on CD-ROM. And since CD-ROM can carry pictures and sound in addition to text, students can see photos, charts, and illustrations to make the material easier to comprehend and retain as well as hearing correct pronunciations, literary, or musical passages. Having sights and sounds in addition to the textual material gives added dimension to the learning process and keeps the student's interest level high.

History is another educational area that benefits from CD-ROM. *United States History* is chronicled on a single CD-ROM that contains the entire text (along with photos, maps and illustrations) of 107 history books. All of our countries major armed conflicts (the Civil War, World War I, World War II, Korea, Vietnam, and Desert Storm) are covered in great detail on CD-ROMs. Desert Storm, the first war viewed in real-time in our living rooms, includes actual recordings of the voices of the reporters who covered the event as well as the military leaders who orchestrated it, augmented by dazzling color photos. The history of the Indians of North America is chronicled on CD-ROM, as is the U.S. space program. There are collections of intelligence information on terrorist groups and CIA data on political climates in the world's hot spots and lots of other fascinating information of all descriptions available on CD-

ROM, too. Specific CD-ROMs are also available that contain collections of impressionist, abstract, and other artistic genres as well.

Art appreciation CD-ROMs bring the collections of the world's greatest galleries and museums to the computer screen. Music is another educational area that benefits from optical media, bringing you right into the world of Beethoven and other great composers, giving you insight and understanding through sight and sound that no mere printed books could ever provide

Nature, animals, and the natural world are also well-covered on CD-ROM, with available titles including John Audubon's complete works on birds and mammals illuminated with his splendid original color illustrations. The National Geographic Society's CD-ROM on mammals includes audio sections that pronounce the animal's name and let you hear what the animal sounds like. Scores of beautiful photographs and several full-motion video segments let you see the animals in action and promote a deeper understanding of the material while presenting it in an enjoyable and entertaining way—what a wonderful way to learn for any age student!

CD-ROM is an excellent medium for learning a foreign language and vocabulary building due to its ability to combine audio with text and graphics. With CD-ROM you can hear the proper pronunciation of a word while seeing how it is spelled, along with graphics that may illustrate its usage.

CD-ROM makes learning skills like sign language and crafts like macramé, origami, weaving, and needlepoint design easier and less stressful to master since the user can proceed at his or her own pace, dwelling on or reviewing material as long or as often as required. CD-ROM and the personal computer combine to make an infinitely patient teacher who never chastises the student, always presents the material in exactly the same way and doesn't mind going over and over it again as often as necessary.

Baseball, the nation's favorite pastime, is also covered on CD-ROM, providing virtually every statistic on just about any player for any team. Cinema devotees will find movie databases on CD-ROM containing still photos, audio samples of actual dialogue, complete cross-referencing of actors, directors, and other production staff for thousands of movies. Aircraft aficionados will find collections of flying machines propelled with jets and props that provide incredibly detailed information on the subject. Computer enthusiasts and programmers have numerous programming references and public domain or shareware software libraries to choose from on CD-ROM.

Genealogy buffs can trace the names and roots of ancestors back for generations on CD-ROM. Bible students can peruse or search the complete and unabridged text of the good book on CD-ROM. Collections of odd, unusual and arcane statistics can be found on CD-ROM, and even the *Guinness Book of Records* is available on optical media. Ghost stories, seals of the U.S. government, classic Hawaiian shirt designs and much, much more is available on CD-ROM. And with new CD-ROM titles being published every day, the information base that is available on optical media is constantly expanding. CD-ROM makes it possible to have the entire contents of a traditional book-based library fit on your desktop. And CD-ROM makes it possible to search, extract, and copy information with facility and speed that could never be realized with ink-and-paper publishing. That's what makes CD-ROM a superior ready-reference medium.

Fun and Games

CD-ROM is also revolutionizing the look, feel, sound, and design of recreational software as well. Thanks to the huge capacity of CD-ROM, computer games can be considerably more complex, include more features, levels, plateaus, and possible scenarios than on magnetic media. Adventure games that allow the user to pursue any of hundreds of possible paths ensure that you'll never play the exact same game twice and thus keep your interest and challenge levels high. Classic games like chess take on a whole new dimension when the knights and pawns actually engage in armed combat, complete with appropriate music and sound effects. CD-ROM makes it possible to eavesdrop on Sherlock Holmes and Dr. Watson as they examine evidence and ponder clues— you can do your own sleuthing and perhaps even solve the cases before Holmes does. Preschoolers and very young children can enjoy hours of wholesome fun that teaches, too, with many of the excellent early learning game CD-ROMs.

Flight simulators and virtual reality programs require many megabytes of disk space, yet don't even come close to taxing the capacity of CD-ROM. We can look forward to recreational software that will continue to get more complex and challenging, with audio and video so realistic that the line between fantasy and reality will become blurred. Multiple-language versions of the same program (such as

English, Spanish, German, French, and Japanese) will easily fit on a single CD-ROM, making the same disc usable in numerous locations around the world.

Medical Reference

Good health is something that everyone is concerned with, and CD-ROM provides valuable information in this area as well. Discs are available that provide information on common maladies and conditions likes minor burns, bruises, colds, sore throats, gout, backache, headaches, and much more along with accepted, effective home remedies for these ailments. Another CD-ROM provides identification and information on virtually every prescription drug legally available in the United States, along with a listing of the possible side effects, other substances that will cause adverse reactions with the drug, usage advisories and so forth.

Special Interests

Special interests are another fertile area for CD-ROM. If you have a penchant for bovine beasts, you might want to use a CD-ROM appropriately named *About Cows*. If you're really into plants and horticulture, *The Plant Doctor* will be a disc that interests you. Just about everything from the monarchs of Europe to a study of erotic art (and even X-rated material) is available on CD-ROM, with more titles being published every day.

Government and Institutional Purposes

Libraries were among the first to realize and utilize the potential of CD-ROM in 1986. The medium's huge capacity and rapid search capabilities make it a natural for library card catalogs where it is many times more efficient than a paper card catalog.

User manuals, training materials, parts catalogs, and technical documents started to appear in CD-ROM format in 1988 as many large companies recognized the advantages that optical media offered. Insurance and investment firms were among the first to use optical media, but other companies soon became converts as well. An employee, agent, dealer, or customer can search for any item, rate, or topic and find it, along with all other information related to it, in seconds using CD-ROM and a computer, reducing the time and effort required to locate information dramatically.

The government of the United States is the country's largest consumer, repository, and distributor of information on a myriad variety of subjects and, as you might expect, uses CD-ROM for many purposes. Various branches of the government use CD-ROM for their own particular requirements since it helps to eliminate or greatly reduce the paper, shipping and storage costs that publishing the same material traditionally would require.

The CIA publishes and deploys volumes of information on CD-ROM to its operatives and agents on the political climates of numerous countries and areas around the world. The Department of Agriculture maintains statistical data on regional rainfall, crop yield, pesticide usage, and more on CD-ROM. The Department of Defense, the FBI, the IRS, and dozens of other federal agencies are all using CD-ROM, and other branches are adopting it as well. From an ecological position, CD-ROM makes sense too, which also enhances its attractiveness to federal agencies. Countless thousands of trees are spared by publishing material on CD-ROM instead of on paper.

Many state and local governments are also finding CD-ROM to be an efficient and cost-effective way of reducing paper usage and maintaining better control over information. Police departments are finding it to be a real boon in searching for suspects, matching fingerprints, correlating data and identifying patterns. CD-ROM is doing its part to take a bite (or megabytes) out of crime.

REVIEW...

CD-ROM...

...can use either text-based or GUI interfaces.

...uses retrieval software to make its data accessible.

...retrieval software differs depending on the disc's content.

...uses the computer's power to search for specific data.

...often permits Boolean operators to make searching even faster and more powerful.

...is much more efficient and cost-effective than paper, microfiche, or other storage mediums.

…can be used for many different purposes from recreation to fighting crime.

…saves trees and helps the ecology by reducing the amount of paper required to store and distribute information.

…helped usher-in the Information Age.

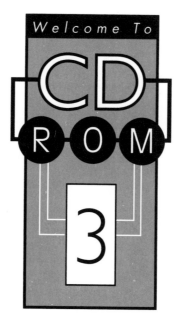

Welcome To **CD ROM**

3

CAN I ADD A CD-ROM DRIVE TO MY PC?

In this lesson...

...CD-ROM hardware requirements

...Differences between Macintosh and IBM-compatible PCs

...SCSI and proprietary interfaces

...PC power and expandability

...Deciding whether to upgrade or replace your PC

...Selecting an internal or external drive

... "Daisychaining" additional drives

... Additional terms and definitions

To use CD-ROM with a personal computer, six distinct components are required:

1. An IBM-compatible or Macintosh computer

2. An interface

3. A CD-ROM drive

4. A connecting cable

5. The required driver software

6. A CD-ROM disc

In response to the question asked in the title of this lesson, "Can I Add a CD-ROM Drive to My PC?", the answer is "yes" if you have item #1 on this list. The computer is the cornerstone of the system, and a CD-ROM drive can be interfaced to virtually any personal computer. The performance of the drive as well as the scope of CD-ROM software you'll be able to access, however, depends to a large degree on the power of the PC itself.

Most desktop PCs are "open systems"—that is, they permit expanding and enhancing the system's configuration by adding additional accessory devices (known as *peripherals*). An interface is the first peripheral component required for adding a CD-ROM drive, so that's where we'll start this lesson.

CD-ROM INTERFACES: THE ESSENTIAL CONNECTING LINK

A CD-ROM drive can't do much of anything on its own. It depends on the computer to give it instructions and to interpret the data it reads from CD-ROM discs. To do this, the CD-ROM drive must be compatibly connected to the PC so the two devices can work harmoniously together. This connection and subsequent communication between the two devices is done via an *interface*.

INTERFACE refers to the point at which two elements in a computer system connect and communicate. Different types of interfaces are present at different levels of computing, ranging from the user interface that enables the user to interact with the computer to the hardware interface that makes connecting external devices to the PC possible.

PROPRIETARY INTERFACES
AND HARDWARE DEPENDENCY

Some CD-ROM drive manufacturers use a proprietary interface to establish communication between the devices, and these interfaces are said to be *hardware dependent* since they are designed to work with a specific CD-ROM drive. Philips, Sony, Hitachi, Matsushita and other manufacturers have all developed their own proprietary interfaces for their CD-ROM drives, although they also have SCSI-interfaced models in their product lines as well.

HARDWARE DEPENDENT means specifically designed and intended for use with a particular hardware device or operating environment. A proprietary-interfaced CD-ROM drive is hardware dependent because it only works with a proprietary interface designed specifically for it and a specific type of computer system. Conversely, a SCSI-interfaced CD-ROM drive is hardware-independent since it works with any computer system that has a SCSI port or interface.

Generally speaking, there is no advantage to using a proprietary interface instead of a SCSI interface, although some manufacturers claim better communication speeds for their proprietary-interfaced drives over the same models equipped with SCSI interfaces instead. Several like devices (the same kind of drives from the same manufacturer) can be connected in a series called *daisychaining*, but devices from other manufacturers can't be intermixed because of the proprietary interfacing. CD-ROM drives that use proprietary interfaces are usually less expensive than SCSI drives, since a separate SCSI interface card must also be purchased separately in addition to the SCSI drive. If cost is a major purchasing consideration then a CD-ROM drive with a proprietary interface may be worth considering, although SCSI interfacing is the preferred format.

THE SCSI SOLUTION

The most popular and widely-accepted interface for CD-ROM drives is the SCSI, an acronym for Small Computer System Interface. SCSI provides a common standard for computer devices to communicate with one another, and SCSI permits the same device to be used with different types of computer systems. For example, the same SCSI CD-ROM drive can be used with a Macintosh, an IBM-compatible personal computer or any other type of computer system that has a SCSI interface port since SCSI provides a common standard for device communication and does not depend on the type of computer or brand of hardware it is used with. SCSI is, therefore, said to be a *hardware independent* interfacing standard.

SCSI (pronounced scuzzy) is an acronym that stands for Small Computer System Interface. SCSI is a standard high-speed parallel interface as defined by the X3T9.2 committee of the American National Standards Institute that permits devices such as CD-ROM drives, hard disks, and printers to be connected to microcomputers.

Up to seven SCSI devices can all be controlled at the same time through a single SCSI interface by interconnecting the devices with cables. Interconnecting several SCSI devices, like connecting multiple proprietary devices, is called *daisychaining*, and permits them all to be controlled by the same interface. Most SCSI CD-ROM drives are equipped with two SCSI ports. The first port is used for attaching the SCSI cable; the second port is used for connecting the daisychain cable from another drive or for inserting a terminator plug.

The first device in a SCSI daisychain is directly connected to the SCSI interface in the computer by a cable. The second device in the daisychain is cable-connected to the first device. The third device is cabled to the second, and so forth as the chain continues until a maximum of seven devices is reached. The last device in the daisychain requires a terminator plug to let the SCSI interface know that this device is the last one in the chain. When there is only one SCSI device connected to the interface a terminator plug is usually not required since many interfaces come equipped with an internal terminator already installed.

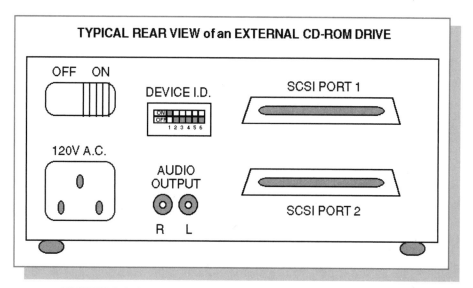

FIGURE 3.1 A typical configuration for the rear panel of an external CD-ROM drive is shown above. The SCSI 1 connector is used for attaching the drive to the PC's SCSI interface, while SCSI 2 is used for connecting a daisychain cable to add another device. If this drive is the last device in a daisychain, then a terminator plug is inserted into SCSI 2 instead to signify that this is the end of the chain. DIP switches are used to set the device identification. The drive in this example has its ID set for Device 1. If all switches are in the off position then Device 0 becomes the ID number.

DAISYCHAINING describes two or more devices linked together through each other to the same PC. The first device is connected directly to the PC, while the second device is connected to the first. The third device is connected to the second, fourth to third, and so forth. Signals are passed through the chain back-and-forth from the computer to the desired device, and to avoid confusion or conflicts, each device in the chain is given its own unique ID.

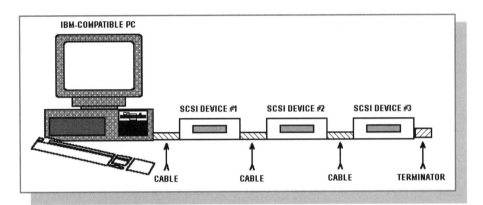

FIGURE 3.2 *An example of daisychaining SCSI devices. The first SCSI device is connected directly to the PC's SCSI interface port by a cable. The second device is cable-connected to the first. The third device is cable-connected to the second, and so on up to a maximum of seven devices total. The last device in the chain has a terminator plug installed that electronically signals the SCSI interface that this is the end of the chain. Each device in the daisychain has its own unique identification number to prevent conflicts with the other devices.*

Each device in a daisychain is given its own unique device identification number so the computer's instructions and signals reach the desired device without affecting any other device in the daisychain. Since all Macintosh computers have a built-in SCSI device, let's use them as an example.

The internal hard disk drive of a Macintosh is always defined as Device 0. A CD-ROM drive daisychained to the Mac would typically be defined as Device 1, while a second (external) hard drive or CD-ROM drive might be defined as Device 3. By giving each device its own unique identification communication conflicts between the computer and the devices are eliminated.

INTERNAL VS. EXTERNAL SCSI INTERFACES

Because the SCSI interface is built-in on the Macintosh, all that is required is to connect the SCSI device to the Mac with a cable and load the appropriate driver software.

Unlike the Macintosh, IBM-compatible computers, however, do not come with a built-in SCSI interface port as standard equipment, so a SCSI interface must be installed and used to establish a connection between the PC and the CD-ROM drive. The two major types of SCSI interfaces are the internal type which must be installed in one of the PC's internal expansion slots, or the external type of SCSI interface, which connects to the PC's parallel printer port. There are some plusses and minuses with both types.

The internal SCSI interface card requires an expansion slot for installation in the PC and the computer must be opened to insert the card. If you have lots of other peripherals (accessory devices) installed on your computer system, you may not have any expansion slots left to install a SCSI interface card in, although most PCs have at least one slot open and available for use. Installing the card entails taking the cabinet cover off the computer system unit to gain access to the expansion slots. While the procedure for installing an interface card is not complicated and doesn't require any technical knowledge or experience, many user's don't feel comfortable with the idea of taking their computer systems apart to install an interface and then reassembling them again. Many computer dealers and repair centers will perform the installation for a nominal fee (or for free if the interface card or CD-ROM drive is purchased from them).

In Lesson 7 the installation of SCSI interfaces on different hardware configurations is described and illustrated to help you decide if doing the installation is a task you'd like to attempt yourself and to guide you through it if you do.

Internal SCSI interfaces are less expensive than external units and provide the best data speed performance. Once they are installed, they don't usually require any additional attention.

External SCSI interfaces don't require opening the computer's case, since they simply plug into the PC's parallel printer port. External SCSI interfaces are also commonly called parallel-to-SCSI interfaces, and they are ideal for use with notebook or laptop computers that usually don't provide any expansion slots to accommodate an internal interface card. They're also a good choice for anyone who doesn't have any vacant slots left in the computer, or who simply doesn't want to install anything internally in their system.

Several different parallel-to-SCSI interfaces are available, and they all plug into the parallel printer port. Some are small self-contained modules slightly thinner than a pack of cigarettes, while others are a bit larger and are equipped with a built-in (as opposed to a detachable) connecting cable. The better parallel-to-SCSI interfaces are *transparent devices* that permit plugging the printer cable into the interface unit so you can still use the printer while the interface is plugged into the parallel port. They are called transparent because they let the printer signals go right through the parallel port without interruption—as if the parallel-to-SCSI interface wasn't there at all.

A TRANSPARENT DEVICE is one that performs its own tasks, usually while sharing a resource such as a system port, without affecting or impeding the operation of any other component in the system. During use, a transparent device is said to be "invisible" to the user since the use is occurring without the user's knowledge.

Parallel-to-SCSI interfaces have slightly slower data transfer speeds than internal SCSI interface cards, but this isn't a major concern for most CD-ROM uses. The slower speed of the external interface, however, may not be desirable for some multimedia CD-ROM applications which feature extensive use of sound and full-motion video or animation. The slower speed of the parallel-to-SCSI interface may cause playback of these sections to seem slightly choppy or jerky rather than completely smooth.

If you select a CD-ROM drive that uses a proprietary interface, you won't have the choice of internal or external interface types. Proprietary interfaces are always internal circuit cards that require an expansion slot in the PC.

INTERNAL VS. EXTERNAL CD-ROM DRIVES

As with the SCSI interfacing, you'll also have to make a choice between an internally-mounted CD-ROM drive or an external unit. The physical layout of your personal computer is a major deciding factor in whether you want an internal or external drive.

Internal CD-ROM drives are half-height units that occupy the same width and height dimensions as a standard 5.25 inch floppy disk drive. If your PC has a vacant 5.25 inch half-height bay and can accommodate the installation of a second disk drive, chances are pretty good that it is able to accommodate an internal CD-ROM drive in this bay instead of another floppy drive.

It is important that the vacant bay be accessible from the front of the PC, since you'll have to be able to insert and remove CD-ROMs from the drive when it is installed. Some PC cabinet configurations provide a "hidden" bay that is not visible from the outside of the machine (sometimes this bay is located toward the rear of the machine) that is perfectly serviceable for mounting a second hard disk drive that does not require any physical user access at all. While this is fine for mounting a hard drive, it is totally unacceptable as the mounting site for a CD-ROM drive.

DEFINITION

A PIGTAIL CONNECTOR is an electrical power connector consisting of a set of four colored wires (one yellow, two black, one red) originating at the PC's power supply that has a socketed white nylon connector at its end. The sockets on this connector mate with contact pins on a internally-mounted drive device (CD-ROM drive, floppy drive, hard drive, or tape backup drive). The nylon connector is "keyed" with slanted corners on two sides that prevents it from being inserted incorrectly.

If your PC's chassis provides an open drive bay, then chances are also pretty good that it's power supply also has an unused pigtail connector to provide the necessary power for a CD-ROM drive, too. A *pigtail* connector is a set of four colored wires (one yellow, two black, one red) originating at the PC's power supply which has a socketed white nylon connector at its end. The sockets on this connector mate with contact pins on the CD-ROM drive (or floppy drive, hard drive, or tape backup drive). The nylon connector is keyed with slanted corners on two sides that prevents it from being inserted incorrectly.

Internal-mount CD-ROM drives have some advantages over external units: they are less expensive (usually $75 to $100) than the same drive in an external cabinet. Since they are permanently installed in and are powered by the host PC they are ready for use whenever the computer is turned on. All cable connections (for power, SCSI and audio) are inside the PC's case making for a neater appearance, and they don't require a separate AC power source since the PC's power supply provides the necessary operating voltage (via the pigtail connector).

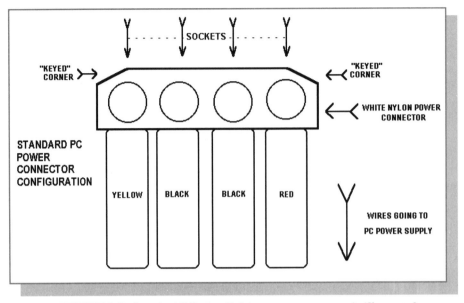

FIGURE 3.3 A typical PC pigtail drive power connector is illustrated above. The keyed corners of the white nylon connector prevent inserting the connector into the CD-ROM drive the wrong way. It only fits when correctly oriented.

If you don't have a front-accessible vacant drive bay available, you'll have to go with an external CD-ROM drive instead of an internally-mounted unit. Most manufacturers offer the same drive in both internal and external configurations. In such cases, the drive itself is identical but the external unit is encased in its own cabinet. In addition to providing a functional and attractive case to house the CD-ROM drive, the cabinet also holds an independent power supply to power the drive (instead of using the PC's power supply via a pigtail connector as is the case with an internal drive). External CD-ROM drives usually cost $75 to $100 more than their internal counterparts, due to the increased manufacturing costs associated with the cabinet and power supply, but offer several advantages that justify their added costs. They don't require an internal drive bay, which can then be used for another internally-mounted device. The same drive can be used with other PC's (or Macintosh computers) by simply plugging it into the desired computer's SCSI port, and device IDs can be changed easily without opening up the computer to get at the ID DIP switches on the drive.

THE HOST PC—CORNERSTONE OF IT ALL

The host PC is the computer system to which the CD-ROM is connected and used. It is called the host because it provides the *services* required to support the CD-ROM drive and the software you use with it, so it acts as a *host* to all of the *guest* devices (including drives of all types, printers, monitor, sound card, and mouse) connected to it.

The **HOST PC** is the main personal computer system that controls and utilizes all other connected devices including drives, printers, monitor, keyboard, mouse, joystick, and more. Since the PC provides the logic, input-output, memory storage, computing, and in many cases the actual operational voltage, the PC hosts the needs of all the devices as if they were guests.

A CD-ROM drive and interface can be installed to work with virtually any IBM-compatible PC starting with the older XT-class machines (based on Intel 8086 CPUs) right through today's high-speed Intel 80486-based powerhouses. All Macintosh Plus, SE, and Series II computers are CD-ROM ready.

CPU is an acronym for Central Processing Unit, which is the "brain" of the computer that actually performs the computations and controls the operations of the machine. In personal computers, the CPUs are also called microprocessors since they are contained entirely on a single chip. The microprocessor can fetch, decode, and execute instructions that enable the computer to do useful work. The CPU is also responsible for the transfer of information to and from other resources (such as RAM and disk drives) that comprise the host computer system.

CPUs AND CD-ROM

A CD-ROM drive is a high-performance device that performs best when connected to a high-performance computer system. By installing a CD-ROM drive on an underpowered PC system, the effect is similar to putting a Corvette engine in a go-cart chassis: you'll never be able to appreciate and use the full power that's available because the other components of the system aren't strong enough, resulting in a mismatch of power. Obsolence as older hardware reaches the end of its useful life due to technological advances is a fact of life when it comes to computers and, sad but true, some of the older PCs are functionally obsolete for today's requirements.

The most basic requirements for a PC to support a CD-ROM drive consist of at least an 8086 CPU, a minimum memory configuration of 512K (kilobytes) of RAM, a hard disk drive, and MS-DOS version 2.11 or later.

A **KILOBYTE** (abbreviated KB, K or Kbyte) is the equivalent of 1,024 bytes. Kilobytes are usually used to express capacities of RAM, floppy diskettes, files, and other measures less than a megabyte (1024x1024=1,048,576 bytes) in size.

RAM, an acronym for Random Access Memory, refers to semiconductor-based (silicon chip-based) memory that can be read and written by the microprocessor or other devices in the computer system. RAM is classified as volatile (rather than stable) memory, since it loses all of its stored data when power is interrupted or removed (the computer is shut off).

While it is indeed possible to support a CD-ROM drive with such a meager configuration, it is not practical. An XT-class system is simply not fast enough or powerful enough to take advantage of either the CD-ROM drive's speed or many of the CD-ROM applications you'll undoubtedly want to run on it.

MS-DOS (pronounced em-ess-doss) is an acronym for Microsoft Disk Operating System. MS-DOS oversees and supervises the basic tasks and services required to run a computer including disk input and output, video support, keyboard control and other essential functions.

If you only intend to do text-based work with the CD-ROM drive, then an XT-class machine might suffice if you absolutely cannot upgrade to a newer model machine with a faster, newer CPU. Be forewarned, how-ever, that using a CD-ROM drive on an XT-class machine proves to be excruciatingly slow and woefully inadequate to run most CD-ROM-based software.

MEGAHERTZ (abbreviated MHz) is a measure of elec-tronic frequency equivalent to one million cycles per sec-ond. The computational speed of a personal computer is dependent on the type and speed of its CPU, as measured in megahertz. A PC with a 12MHz CPU is oscillating at twice the speed of the same PC with a 6MHz microproces-sor of the same type.

The minimum practical system that should be considered is an 80286-based PC running at a speed of at least 12MHz and equipped with at least 1MB of RAM. A hard disk drive, a VGA video card and color monitor, and MS-DOS version 3.3 or later are also basic requirements for spartan, utili-tarian uses with CD-ROM.

VGA, an acronym for Video Graphics Array, is a video adapter introduced in 1987 by IBM. VGA provides moder-ately high-resolution screen images up to a maximum of 640 horizontal pixels by 480 vertical pixels in either two or six-teen colors from a 262,144-color palette. VGA's low-resolu-tion mode provides screen-image resolution of 320 horizontal pixels by 200 vertical pixels with 256 colors simul-taneously displayable from the same 262,144-color palette. VGA is the minimum video standard that should be consid-ered for CD-ROM applications, with SVGA being preferable.

SVGA, an acronym for Super VGA, is a superset of the original VGA specification which yields higher resolution. 640x480/256-color, 800x600 and 1024x768 resolutions are all considered to be SVGA operational modes and are gaining popularity rapidly. SVGA is preferred for any intensely graphic applications and is particularly well-suited for CD-ROM.

While this is still far from being the preferred configuration, this system permits running most CD-ROM software (albeit a bit slower than you'd like) and also supports a minimum Microsoft Windows environment. This is an important consideration, as more and more CD-ROM titles are being created to run under the Windows GUI environment.

A **MEGABYTE** (abbreviated MB) is the term used to represent 1,048,576 bytes (1,024x1,024 bytes). Megabytes are used to represent large capacities when referring to total system RAM memory, large disk drives, and CD-ROM data capacities.

In realistic terms you really shouldn't consider using CD-ROM on any system that isn't based on a 16MHz or faster 80386 microprocessor with 2MB or more RAM, an 80MB or larger hard drive, a VGA adapter and color monitor, a mouse, MS-DOS 4.01 or later, and Microsoft Windows if you really want to get the most performance and enjoyment from optical media. As with everything else related to computing, the more processing power, speed and memory available the better the overall performance of the system will be. A faster and more powerful CPU, additional RAM, a higher capacity hard drive, and a Super VGA adapter with multiscan color monitor helps you to more easily realize the full potential and benefit that CD-ROM has to offer.

Prices of personal computers continue to drop as their power and features increase dramatically, making this an ideal time to consider upgrading your PC if you don't already own a 386 or 486 machine. As applications become larger and more complex more speed and computing power is required to run these programs at an acceptable speed. In a very practical sense it can be said that the XT-class machine is already dead, and the 286-based system is gasping its last desperate breaths of life. Many people feel that even 386-based systems running at speeds under 25MHz are impractical for use in today's GUI application environments. These are all valid points that you should consider before deciding to purchase and install a CD-ROM drive and interface in a machine that may already be outmoded and past its useful prime.

If you decide that purchasing a newer, more powerful PC as the base platform for your CD-ROM system makes sense, you should seriously consider a 486-based machine, since the price difference between the entry-level 486s (such as 80486SX/25MHz systems) and a 386/33MHz system is only a little more and it buys a lot more computing power and speed. Even though the 386 system may run at a higher speed, the

486SX has more internal computing power so it calculates in less time than the 386 system.

Many computer dealers and mail-order computer outlets allow you to order a system with a CD-ROM drive already installed, and this approach makes sense for those users who want a ready-to-use CD-ROM system right out of the box. Another advantage of ordering a system with a CD-ROM drive installed is that everything is already in place, tested, and operational before it is shipped. Tandy/Radio Shack and other major manufacturers are also offering CD-ROM drives as part of the standard equipment on some of their 386 and 486 models.

SEVEN QUESTIONS TO ASSESS YOUR SYSTEM AND REQUIREMENTS

Here's a checklist you can use in determining whether you should consider adding a CD-ROM drive to your present PC or upgrade the entire system. It also helps you decide what type of interface and drive is right for your system as well. Get a sheet of paper and answer the following questions.

Question 1: What type of microprocessor does my system have and what is its speed?

Points to consider: An XT-class (8086) machine, regardless of its speed, will not deliver the performance you'll require of it for CD-ROM work. An AT-class (80286) machine running at 12MHz or faster may be serviceable for limited CD-ROM applications but you'll undoubtedly need (and want) more speed and power. A 386 machine running at 16MHz or faster gives satisfactory performance for most applications. A 486 system yields the best speed and performance, with the fastest 486 CPUs being the most desirable.

Question 2: How much RAM does my system have and can it be expanded?

Points to consider: While 640K of RAM may be enough for DOS-based CD-ROMs, it won't be enough to run Windows or any of the CD-ROMs that are designed for that environment (the number of Windows-based CD-ROM titles is growing faster than any other segment). Most AT-class machines permit expansion up to 2MB or 4MB of RAM directly on the motherboard by adding either DRAM chips or SIMMs.

MOTHERBOARD is the main circuit board containing the primary "system critical" components for a microcomputer system. The components that are found on the motherboard include the CPU, main memory, controller circuitry required for the expansion bus and expansion slots in addition to other components required for the proper operation of these circuits.

DEFINITION

Consider the cost of purchasing and installing additional RAM and add this to the cost of the drive and interface kit to calculate your projected expenditure. Remember, too, that a 286-based system has a limited lifespan in today's computing environment. 386- and 486-based systems can typically accommodate expansion to 8MB or more using SIMMs, and this is more than adequate for all but the most demanding power user applications.

Question 3: Do I have a drive bay available?

Points to consider: An internal-mount CD-ROM drive has the same physical dimensions as a half-height floppy or hard disk drive, and thus requires a standard half-height drive bay. This bay must be located at the front of the PC chassis, however, so you'll have access to it from the front of the machine for inserting and removing CD-ROMs from the drive. If no half-height, front-accessible drive bay is available you have to purchase an external CD-ROM drive.

Question 4: Do I have a vacant expansion slot available?

Points to consider: An internal CD-ROM interface requires an expansion slot for insertion, whether it is a proprietary or SCSI interface. If your PC has no vacant slots or if you have a laptop or notebook computer that does not have any expansion slots, you won't be able to use an internal interface card, thus effectively removing a proprietary-interfaced drive as a candidate for your consideration. External parallel-to-SCSI interfaces can be used for SCSI CD-ROM drives, since they simply plug into the PC's printer port, and this is the way to go for these systems.

Question 5: Can my PC's power supply support a CD-ROM drive?

Points to consider: If your PC has at least one vacant drive bay available it probably also has at least one available pigtail power connector that can supply the required operational voltage for the CD-ROM drive. This is only important if you are considering an internal CD-ROM drive, since external drives have their own independent power supplies built-into their cabinet housings. A 200-watt power supply should be considered the minimum capacity for any internal CD-ROM drive installation.

Question 6: What operating system version am I using?

Points to consider: MS-DOS has undergone several major revisions and improvements over the years. For that reason, the latest version is the most desirable. With the release of MS-DOS version 4.01 support for high-capacity storage devices was directly implemented (prior to this version a 32MB limitation existed which meant that only the first 32MB of any volume could be accessed directly). As of this writing MS-DOS 5.0 is the currently-available version, although MS-DOS 6.0 is now undergoing beta testing and may be available by the time you read this.

Question 7: Can my PC handle GUIs?

Points to consider: Microsoft Windows has attracted a huge user base as the graphical user interface of choice for thousands of applications. It readily lends itself to CD-ROM, since it was designed to accommodate the medium right from the start.

WINDOWS, the popular name for Microsoft Windows, is a multitasking graphical user interface environment that runs on MS-DOS-based computers. Drop-down menus, screen windows, and icons that represent entire programs or specific tasks are all features of Windows that makes most computer tasks simply a matter of pointing with a mouse and clicking one of the mouse buttons to activate that application or utility.

To run Windows or DOS-based applications that make use of GUIs you'll need a mouse for pointing and clicking, a VGA monitor (or SVGA) and at least 2MB of RAM with a 286 or higher CPU (386 or 486 is desirable). Unless you intend to restrict your CD-ROM usage to text-only databases, GUI capability is essential.

REVIEW...

CD-ROM...

...requires 6 distinct components to be present:

1. An IBM-compatible or Macintosh computer.
2. An interface.
3. A CD-ROM drive.
4. A connecting cable.
5. The required driver software.
6. A CD-ROM disc.

...requires a fast CPU and sufficient RAM memory to operate properly.

...is best used with 80386- or 80486-based PCs.

...requires a front-accessible drive bay for internal mounting.

...can be used with a parallel-to-SCSI interface if no internal slots are available.

...external drives generally cost $75 to $100 more than internal drives of the same specification.

...spending a bit more on a 486-machine is a better long-term investment.

...installing a CD-ROM drive isn't rocket science and most users are able to perform an installation with no special tools or skills.

Welcome To

CD ROM

4

MPC
THE MULTIMEDIA STANDARD

In this lesson...

...MPC—The Merging of Sound and Pictures

...The MPC Marketing Council and Standards

...How MPC-capable CD-ROM drives differ

...Additional terms and definitions

Multimedia—the merging of text, audio, and graphics—is the newest dimension of personal computing and, thanks to the wide acceptance of the Windows graphical operating system, one that is gaining in popularity at an amazingly fast rate.

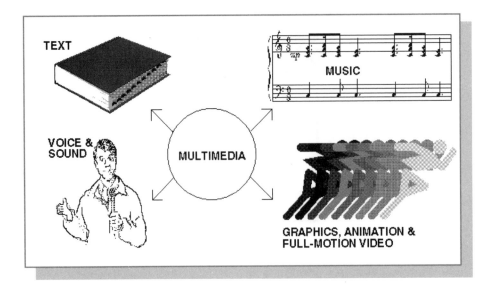

FIGURE 4.1 Multimedia merges text, music, voice narratives, recorded sounds, graphics, animation, and full-motion video together on CD-ROM. Because of the vast amounts of information that are involved in multimedia presentations, CD-ROM drives with fast access and data-transfer speeds and large buffers are required for satisfactory playback.

Multimedia isn't a new idea, but until the higher speed and power of 386- and 486-based PCs with lots of RAM memory became readily available it wasn't an idea that could easily be implemented. These faster PCs, coupled with the huge capacity of CD-ROM, make full-blown presentations possible, affordable, and relatively easy to produce for the average PC user.

Some standard specification was needed to define just what hardware requirements would constitute the necessary elements to produce multimedia on personal computers.

FIGURE 4.2 *The MPC trademark logo, shown above, is the identification mark to look for on multimedia products and packaging. While the term multimedia applies to a number of new computer technologies on the market today, only products bearing this logo are certified by the Multimedia PC Marketing Council as being compliant with its MPC specifications. Look for it when considering a purchase.*

The Multimedia PC Marketing Council, a subsidiary of the Software Publishers Association, was formed to establish a set of technical specifications for multimedia hardware products that is being widely adopted in the PC industry. The intention was to establish standards for producing products that feature *plug-and-play* simplicity for consumers as well as to help develop the marketplace quickly for products that comply with these specifications. Products that do comply are identified by the MPC logo on the packaging. The right to use the MPC trademark logo on a product is granted after the product has been approved and certified by the Council.

The three principal components of MPC are the host PC, a sound/audio device, and a multimedia-capable CD-ROM drive, although other components are also included in the specification. Here's an abridged version of the MPC Hardware Specifications Version 1.0, presented here in the interest of completeness:

...**CPU.** The minimum requirement is a 386SX or compatible microprocessor.

...**RAM.** The minimum requirement is 2MB of extended memory.

...**Video**. VGA-compatible display adapter and a color VGA-compatible monitor.

...**Input Devices**. A 101-key IBM-style keyboard with standard DIN connector or a keyboard that delivers identical functionality utilizing key combinations, a two-button mouse with a bus or serial connector, and at least one additional communication port remaining free.

A **DIN CONNECTOR** is a round, multipin connector that conforms to the German national standards organization specification (Deutsch Industrie Norm). DIN connectors are usually used for connecting the keyboard to the PC's main system unit, and the most frequent configurations are either 5- or 8-pin connectors.

...**I/O**. A standard 9- or 25-pin asynchronous serial port, programmable up to 9600 baud, switchable interrupt channel; a standard 25-pin bi-directional parallel port with interrupt capability; 1 MIDI port with input, output and throughput capability with interrupt support for input and FIFO transfer; and an IBM-style analog or digital joystick port.

...**MPC System Software**. MPC system software must conform to APIs, function and performance described in the Microsoft Windows Software Development Kit Programmer's Reference, Volumes I and II (Version 3.0) and the Microsoft Multimedia Development Kit Programmer's Reference (Beta version, published November 15, 1992 and due to be updated at the final release of the Multimedia Development Kit).

API, an abbreviation for Application Programming Interface, is a set of routines that an application program uses to request and execute low-level services performed by the PC's operating system.

...**CD-ROM**. The drive must be capable of a sustained 150Kb-per-second data transfer rate with an average seek time of 1 second or less. The drive must also provide Mode 1 audio capability and an MSCDEX 2.2x (Microsoft CD Extensions) driver that implements extended audio APIs (Application Programming Interfaces).

MSCDEX, an acronym for Microsoft CD Extensions, is the system-level driver software from Microsoft that extends the normal capabilities of the MS-DOS operating system to utilize CD-ROM. As of this writing the current version of MSCDEX is 2.21. The MSCDEX.EXE file is normally included as a line in the AUTOEXEC.BAT file and loaded automatically when the PC is booted.

The drive cannot consume more than 40 percent of the CPU bandwidth while maintaining a sustained transfer rate of 150KB per second. The drive must provide CD-DA (Red Book) audio outputs and have a front-mounted volume control.

MODE 1 is an encoding scheme used in producing CD-ROM which utilizes three layers of error detection and correction for maintaining the integrity of computer data (text, numbers, and so on).

MODE 2 is an encoding scheme used in producing CD-ROM that provides two layers of error detection and correction, used most often with audio or compressed audio/video data (such as sound or full-motion video).

RED BOOK is the standard specification for CD Audio as detailed and agreed upon by Philips, Sony and other major manufacturers. Since these technical specifications were published in a book with a red cover, this specification for audio became known as the Red Book standard. The letters CD-DA (Compact Disc-Digital Audio) are also used frequently in reference to the Red Book specification as well.

Additional information on the technical specifications required for hardware compliance are available upon request from the Multimedia PC Marketing Council, 1730 M Street NW, Suite 700, Washington, DC 20036.

MULTIMEDIA-CAPABLE VS. STANDARD CD-ROM DRIVES

The main things that set MPC drives apart from non-MPC drives are data transfer speed and buffer size. In short, MPC drives can transfer data at a minimum sustained rate of 150KB/second and they have larger buffers.

The buffer size is important for smooth playback of animation, full-motion video, multimedia presentations and other uses where large volumes of data must be retrieved from the CD-ROM drive and delivered to the PC in a smooth, continuous flow without interruption.

Multimedia-capable CD-ROM drives usually have 64KB buffers, as opposed to the 16 or 32KB buffers usually found in non-MPC drives. The larger buffer provides a temporary "holding area" for retrieved data while the drive is busy locating and transferring the next chunk of information that will be needed by the application. Having a large buffer makes it possible to stockpile the data faster than the PC can empty the buffer, so there is never an interruption to the flow.

Now, while most drives are capable of transferring data at the rate of 150KB per second, this may not be fast enough to keep the buffer and the host PC "fed" and some gaps, choppiness, or interruptions to the presentation may occur. To combat this occurrence, many drive manufacturers are producing drives that can read data at double the standard transfer rate. Not surprisingly, these drives also usually have faster access times and higher price tags as well.

Deciding whether to go with a standard CD-ROM drive or an MPC model depends on two factors: your intended uses for the drive and how much money you can spend on the purchase.

Some manufacturers, like NEC, offer upgrades for their older drives to modernize them. Under NEC's program, you can return an older NEC drive to be upgraded for a nominal charge. The upgrade consists of replacing some of the electronic components including buffer RAM chips to make the drive suitable for multimedia uses. What's attractive about this upgrade program is that the cost of an upgrade is substantially lower than purchasing a new drive, so if you already own an older CD-ROM drive you should contact the manufacturer to find out if it can be upgraded.

Bear in mind that as CD-ROM software continues to evolve the applications and programs provided on this medium will continue to become larger and more complex. A drive with a faster data transfer speed and a larger buffer will be an asset, so spending a little extra for a multimedia-capable drive is a good long-term investment.

While shopping for a drive you'll also see the term CD-ROM/XA-compatible used in the descriptions of some drives. The XA designation stands for Extended Architecture which is a design standard jointly developed by Philips, Sony, and Microsoft. The particular benefits of XA are that it permits freely mixing both Mode 1 and Mode 2 data sources on the same CD to produce extended play times and the simultaneous display of moving video and graphics while digital audio is being processed. CD-ROM/XA discs can also be played on a CD-I player as well as on a standard CD-ROM drive.

The XA designation is somewhat of a dark horse at the present time, however, since a special XA controller card is required to realize any of the potential benefits this extended standard has to offer. Software conforming to this extended architecture hasn't been produced in large quantities, and consequently, the XA designation shouldn't be a deciding factor in your choice of a drive unless you have very specific application requirements that must have this capability to function properly.

CD-ROM/XA—the XA designation stands for Extended Architecture which uses both Mode 1 and Mode 2 (X/A). By mixing both modes on the same CD-ROM, low- to medium-fidelity audio can be simultaneously processed while data is viewed. The X/A standard was jointly developed and announced by Philips, Sony and Microsoft in August 1988. CD-ROM/XA discs can be played on a CD-I player as well as on a standard CD-ROM player, but a CD-ROM X/A controller card is required in the PC to access X/A capabilities.

REVIEW...

Multimedia...

...combines text, graphics, sound, and full-motion video.

...is the hottest software development area and CD-ROM is playing a major part in it.

...is feasible and practical thanks to fast 386 and 486 PCs.

...has a standard specification set forth by the Multimedia PC Marketing Council, a subsidiary of the Software Publishers Association.

...products that are certified to comply with this specification are granted the right to use the MPC logo trademark on the product and packaging.

...CD-ROM drives with larger buffers and faster access/data transfer speeds are better for multimedia applications.

...some older CD-ROM drives can be upgraded for multimedia.

...multimedia-capable CD-ROM drives cost more than standard drives but are a better long-term investment.

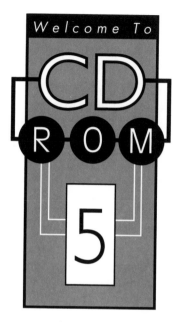

OTHER CD-ROM FORMATS

In this lesson...

...Philips CD-I
...Kodak Photo CD
...Tandy/Memorex VIS
...Sony Multimedia Player
...Commodore CDTV
...Other Special Formats
...Additional terms and definitions

It's often amazing how quickly a good idea catches on, either in its original form or with some modifications to make it appealing to the masses. CD-ROM is an excellent example of a good idea that has been "massaged" into a form that makes it appealing to the average consumer.

CD-ROM, in the sense I've been referring to it throughout this book, requires interfacing to a personal computer system before any useful work can be done. The problem in making CD-ROM a true mass-market product, therefore, is that the majority of people don't have a personal computer in their homes.

The product-marketing gurus reasoned that if the computer could be removed from the equation, or at least from visibility, then CD-ROM would become a mass-marketable product, especially if it could be connected to a television set for viewing and used by the whole family.

The product-design teams at several different companies all came up with similar machines, but the formats of the media they use differ as do the means used to access it. Their common element is that they all permit viewing on a standard color television set and they all have the ability to play audio CDs as well.

This chapter is being included here because these machines, though only breaking into the marketplace as this book is being written, are already attracting lots of media and consumer attention and, I'm sure, will become as commonplace in American households within the next three years as VCRs are today. That may happen even sooner, since these specialized CD-ROM players are much easier to use than the average VCR is, and that's a key element in gaining public acceptance and success in the sales arena.

Compatibility of the media between machines is a big issue, and not one that will be resolved in the foreseeable future, so that should be a major consideration if you're thinking of purchasing one of these machines. While all of these machines can play audio CDs, they can't use dedicated media interchangeably. What that means, simply, is that a disc designed for the Philips CD-I player won't work on the Tandy/Memorex VIS player or vice versa. More importantly, if you're thinking of getting double-duty from your computer CD-ROMs by playing them in one of these players connected to your TV set (regardless of which one it might be), you can forget that notion. None of these consumer-level players can read or display information written for computer CD-ROM use (ISO

9660 or Macintosh HFS data formats), except for the limited capabilities of the Sony MMCD machine to read text-based material.

The following compatibility table will hopefully aid you in understanding what kind of media will and will not work with a specific machine.

TABLE 5.1 Media format incompatibility between the various players is a serious issue to consider when contemplating a purchase.

DATA FORMATS	CD-ROM DRIVES (PC OR MAC)	PHILIPS CD-I	KODAK PHOTO CD	MEMOREX VIS	MULTIMEDIA PLAYER	COMMODORE CDTV
CD-Audio	Yes	Yes	Yes	Yes	Yes	Yes
Photo CD	Some models	Yes	Yes	No	No	No
HS/ISO 9660	Yes	No	No	No	Some titles	No
Mac HFS	Yes	No	No	No	No	No
CD+G	Audio only	Yes	Yes	Yes	Audio only	Yes
CDTV	No	No	No	No	No	Yes
CD-I	No	Yes	Yes	No	No	No
VIS	No	No	Yes	Yes	No	No
CD-ROM/XA	Some models	No	No	No	Yes	No

DEFINITION

MULTI-SESSION/SINGLE-SESSION—these are terms that pertain to the Kodak Photo CD. Single-session Photo CDs are discs that have had all of their images transferred onto them in one single session, and one table of contents for the disc is generated. Multi-session Photo CDs contain images that were transferred during several different sessions, with each subsequent session generating its own table of contents for that session. The ability of CD-ROM drives and other consumer-level devices to read these discs varies from product to product. A drive is said to be single-session capable if it can display the images listed on the disc's single table of contents. A drive (or device) is multi-session capable if it can read and display the images contained in all directories in the table of contents (single session drives only display the images of the original TOC if a multi-session Photo CD is being used).

Now let's learn more about each of these machines designed to play other CD-ROM formats.

KODAK PHOTO CD

Kodak took a unique approach to their CD-ROM player, devoting it entirely to the playback of Kodak's proprietary-format Photo CDs and to playing standard audio CDs.

The device connects directly to a television set and, optionally, a stereo system. The Kodak Photo CD Player only reads audio CDs or Photo CDs that have been produced by Kodak through its participating photofinishers. No other CD-ROM format is recognized or capable of being used by this machine.

The Photo CD discs contain photographs taken with ordinary cameras and film that are scanned and transferred onto the optical media using one of Kodak's writable CD systems such as the Kodak PCD Writer 200. The scanning and transferal can be done either at Kodak's facilities or at a local photofinisher if suitably equipped.

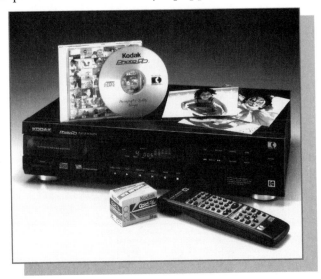

FIGURE 5.1 *The Kodak Photo CD Player (Model PCD 870 shown above) plays back Photo CD images on any television set as well as providing high-fidelity stereo playback for audio CDs. Photo CD Master discs can contain sound, text, and graphics, as well as photo images.*

Up to 100 images (four 24-exposure rolls of film) can be contained on a Kodak Photo CD, and these images are in several formats that make them accessible for viewing on several different CD-ROM reading devices, including some of the newer computer CD-ROM drives. The image resolution of the scanned images is sixteen times greater than today's TV standards and four times greater than the standards currently being considered for HDTV. This seeming over-abundance of image data results in pristine images with sparkling clarity and brilliant, lifelike colors.

One of the main reasons for this ultra-high-resolution scanning is that the Photo CD Master disc can also function as a "digital negative" so you can take the disc to your favorite photofinisher and have prints made of the desired images.

When viewed using the Kodak Photo CD Player connected to a television set, the image display is controlled via a wireless remote controller. The viewer can select specific images, program them to appear in a particular order, rotate the image or zoom-in on part of it for a close-up look.

As of this writing Kodak is presently offering three Photo CD player models, each of which has full stereophonic high-fidelity audio capability in addition to a unique set of picture-viewing functions.

The first is a low-priced player with basic picture-viewing and basic audio CD features. It allows the viewer to delete some pictures from the playback sequence and to keep others. It can also remember the changes, which eliminates the need to program a disc each time it is viewed. An "autoplay" feature allows the player to automatically sequence through selected images at intervals of two seconds.

A deluxe player is also offered that provides a variety of more advanced viewing options in addition to the audio play features. Users can view close-ups of their images, selecting a rectangular portion for magnification with a 2X tele feature. Another feature, called the expanded favorite picture selection, provides additional memory for recalling the individual picture edits and viewing order selections of more discs.

The third model in Kodak's Photo CD player line offers all of the advanced features of the deluxe version but also adds a five-disc carousel serving mechanism. This player also provides on-screen display of the selected image number for easy indexing and fast photo identification.

Intended primarily as a bridging mechanism to help consumers make the inevitable transition from film-based photography to totally electronic imaging, the Kodak Photo CD players and Photo CD discs successfully merge the brilliance and clarity of photography with the digital image processing capabilities of CD-ROM.

PC and Macintosh users with CD-ROM drives capable of reading Photo CD discs can manipulate, enhance, export, and use their Photo CD images with their computer applications as well. Kodak has five software products available for working with Photo CD images on the computer.

...**Photo CD Access** software is available for DOS/Windows and Macintosh operating system users. This basic software utility provides the ability to read and save Photo CD images.

...**PhotoEdge** image enhancement and correction software lets users do more advance image correction and improvement.

...**Browser** software is a basic image database package that allows easy keyword search and retrieval. This software is only available on Kodak's new Photo CD Catalog discs, and it comes included as a standard feature of these discs.

...**Shoebox** image search and retrieval database software expands on the capabilities of Browser software, offering more powerful database functions for users who need to search through large numbers of stored images.

...**Renaissance** design software is an intuitive page-layout package that has been upgraded to allow the direct input of Photo CD images.

PHILIPS CD-I

Philips CD-I is another proprietary format. CD-I stands for *Compact Disc—Interactive*. Philips is the company responsible for the development of the compact disc as well as the audio cassette and, as such, is a recognized and respected company in the electronics industry known for innovative and revolutionary products. The Philips CD-I player has already made a noticeable impact on the consumer marketplace since its release in November, 1992.

Compact Disc—Interactive is an excellent name for the format, since it succinctly describes what it is and what it does: It is a CD-ROM that behaves according to the user's interaction with it.

FIGURE 5.2 *The Philips CDI-910 CD-Interactive Player is shown above. In addition to playing all audio CDs in full hi-fi stereo, the machine can also play Kodak Photo CDs and CD+G discs. A joystick is built into the wireless remote controller for making user interaction possible. A wired trackball controller, available as an accessory, is better for gameplay than the wireless remote.*

The CD-I player connects directly to a television set and it can also connect to a stereo system if desired. The Philips CD-I player also provides full high fidelity stereophonic playback of audio CDs.

A wireless remote controller provides the means for the user to interact with the CD-I software and control certain functions of the CD-I player. The remote unit has buttons for clicking on a control function, ejecting the disc, and performing other functions, which include adjusting the audio volume.

A miniature joystick, also built into the wireless remote, is used to control the on-screen cursor arrow displayed on the television set. An optional trackball controller which cable-connects to a jack on the CD-I player is also available as an accessory item. The trackball is easier for youngsters to use and is much more responsive for high-speed operation of some CD-I software titles like action games.

Not surprisingly, Philips has attracted a substantial number of software developers and publishers to support the CD-I format, and as of this writing there are about 100 software titles available, with more on the way in a continuous stream.

While researching this machine, I had the occasion to use several of the CD-I titles including *Compton's Interactive Encyclopedia, Smithsonian Treasures, Caesar's World of Gambling, A Visit to the Amparo Museum, American Treasures, Gifts to Behold, Gardening by Choice, Private Lessons: Classical Guitar, Private Lessons: Jazz Guitar, Pinball* and *Escape from CyberCity.* All of these titles were indeed interactive to one degree or another. For example, the *Amparo Museum* and *Treasures of the Smithsonian* require relatively little interactivity once you select a topical section for presentation. *Pinball* and *CyberCity* both require constant interaction from the user. The amount of interactivity is determined both by the disc's content and the user's activity level.

Interactivity with the CD-I system, as with any of the other machines that do not directly interact and depend on a PC, is limited to the *possibility paths* that are programmed into the software. For example, if you "walk" down the main corridor of a museum via a CD-I disc, you are only permitted to go to the right or left when the program has provisions for branching in that direction. Access to the information contained on the CD-I disc is limited to what the programmers have permitted. All choices on CD-I discs are made by moving the on-screen cursor arrow to the desired selection and pressing one of the action buttons (which have the same effect as pressing Return or Enter on a computer keyboard). Keeping the design of the CD-I player simple also dictated making the software applications equally simple to operate, which, in turn, affects the interactivity level of the disc.

The picture quality and stereo sound of the CD-I player is quite good, and the animation and interactivity makes using the applications fun and easy. Users can look forward to seeing lots of titles for this machine on dealers shelves, with many more to follow as the CD-I format gains popularity and support.

TANDY/MEMOREX MD-2500 VIS

Another proprietary-format of CD-ROM is the Video Information System (VIS) developed by Memorex and being manufactured, marketed, and distributed by Tandy Corporation and its Radio Shack stores.

The VIS player is connected directly to a television set and, optionally, to a stereo system for full high-fidelity stereophonic playback of both audio CDs and VIS format discs.

The machine is also capable of playing CD+G discs (these are audio CDs that also have some graphic information imbedded on them). The VIS player, however, cannot play Kodak Photo CDs in either their single-session or multi-session formats, nor is it capable of playing CD-I discs, CD/XA discs, or computer (HFS or ISO 9660) CD-ROMs.

The VIS dedicated format has attracted lots of attention and support from software developers, however, for two reasons. The first is that Tandy is a major manufacturing and marketing force, with nearly 7,000 stores and an exceptionally loyal customer base. The second reason for the attention the VIS player is receiving from the software development community is that it is, in fact, a DOS-based machine on the programming level which makes it a relatively easy and speedy task to convert existing DOS CD-ROM code to conform with the VIS specification and interactive interface requirements. The result is a rich assortment of software that was released simultaneously with the VIS player, as well as an ongoing stream of additional titles. As of this writing approximately fifty software and publishing companies have committed to delivering over 100 VIS titles that will have suggested retail prices of $29.95 to $79.95.

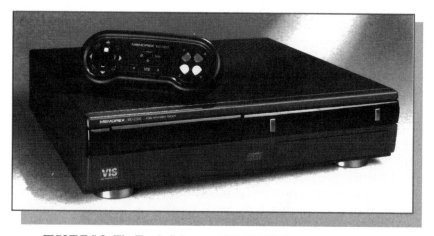

FIGURE 5.3 *The Tandy/Memorex MD-2500 VIS player is really a DOS-based PC wearing consumer electronics clothing. The machine is capable of playing audio CDs and CD+G discs in addition to the proprietary VIS format. The player's unique Save-It cartridge retains scores, bookmark and other pertinent user information for recall at a later session.*

A wireless remote controller is provided with the unit for interacting with the software. A rocker-type switch mechanism is used rather than a joystick for directional control, while a slide-selector switch is used for selecting solo or two-player action. A four-button control pad is also built into the hand control unit. The controller is ergonomically shaped to fit the hand's contours, so even youngsters may use it without difficulty.

Options for the VIS include a second cable-connected hand controller for head-to-head play action. A modem is also available for connecting with on-line information services.

A unique feature of the VIS is the *Save-It* cartridge included with the player. This cartridge provides a means of saving game scores, preserving electronic bookmarks in reference books and saving other user-selected information for recall and use at a later time.

The MD-2500 CD-I player comes with a specially-designed VIS version of the entire twenty-six-volume *Compton's Multimedia Encyclopedia*, which includes a complete *Webster's Intermediate Dictionary* on the same disc. This bundled title contains thousands of colorful illustrations, excellent animated sequences, and digital sound and speech.

In addition to the Compton's disc packed along with the player, I also had the opportunity to work with several VIS software titles while researching this chapter, and they included: *Atlas of U.S. Presidents*, the *Great Lives Series* (Vol. 1), *American Vista, World Vista, Sherlock Holmes: Consulting Detective* (Vols. I and II), *Time Table of History: Business, Politics, and Media*, the *American Heritage Illustrated Encyclopedia and Dictionary, SmartKids Challenge One Games*, eight of the *Kids Read* titles, *Rick Ribbit's Adventures in Early Learning, Rainbow & Snowflake's Search for the Sea* and two *Henry and Mudge* story titles.

Many of the titles, as you can see, are intended for youngsters ages four and up. They are excellent educational products that teach preschooler's and youngsters while holding their attention for hours. The interactivity of the programs permit progressing at a pace that's comfortable for the child, and the ability to control the events happening on screen (to one degree or another) is also a very attractive element to children, since they have to depend on grown-ups for just about everything else.

Several of the current titles as well as those yet to be released are appealing to all members of the family, with the *Compton's Multimedia Encyclopedia* disc as a good representative example.

FIRMWARE is software instructions, such as start-up routines, low-level input/output instructions, and so forth, which are stored in read-only memory (ROM). Unlike RAM (random access memory), which "forgets" all that is contained in it when power is removed, ROM "remembers" all that is programmed into it, making it ideal for instructions and information that is needed by the device on a permanent basis.

The MD-2500 VIS has an MS-DOS-based computer as its heart, and as such, has some inherent advantages over some of the other machines. The principal advantage is that additional capabilities can be given to the machine when upgraded firmware becomes available. An example of this may include an upgrade that gives the machine the ability to read other formats it is not presently able to read, such as Photo CD. The *Save-It* cartridge gives this hardware platform additional flexibility with the ability to retain and recall information based on user activity. Because of these factors, the future looks reasonably bright for the VIS.

SONY MULTIMEDIA PLAYER

Sony, another major technological product development and consumer-electronics company, has taken yet another proprietary approach in making CD-ROM practical for the mass consumer with its portable Multimedia Player.

A radical departure in form and format from the Kodak Photo CD player, the Philips CD-I, and the Tandy/Memorex VIS, the Sony Multimedia Player is small enough to carry around with you and has its own display screen built-in, making it a totally portable, independent unit.

The player is only 7 inches wide, 2 inches high and 6 inches long and only weights two pounds. Since it also plays audio CDs and has an audio jack for stereo headphones or small Walkman-type speakers, this unit is sure to become a favorite leisure-time device for listening to audio CDs when it's not being used for data-retrieval uses.

The Multimedia Player is capable of reading CD-ROM/XA discs that conform to its data format requirements. Additional format capabilities may be offered in later versions of the unit, or as optional upgrades.

LCD, an abbreviation for liquid crystal display, is a type of display that uses a liquid compound having a structure that makes different character patterns visible when electrical voltage is applied to it. Many wristwatches and portable consumer electronics devices use LCD displays.

The device integrates a CD-ROM drive that supports the CD-ROM/XA standard, a PC-compatible microprocessor (the operating system is on ROM), an LCD display panel, a speaker, a keyboard, and a cursor pad all in a compact unit small enough to fit inside a briefcase.

The Multimedia Player can also be connected directly to a color television and it is also equipped with a serial port. The serial port can be used for outputting information to a printer, uploading information to a personal computer or, with the proper software, connecting to a modem.

Sony's stature in the electronics and computer industries, as well as its highly-respected reputation for quality products in the consumer marketplace assures the Multimedia Player a promising future. Major software developers and publishers including Axxis Electronic Publishing, Compact Publishing Inc., Compton's New Media, Random House, and IBM all have announced their intentions of releasing titles that are compatible with the Sony Multimedia Player.

COMMODORE CDTV

CDTV stands for Commodore Dynamic Total Vision, a proprietary CD-ROM format designed by and for Commodore computers. The CDTV player has a Commodore Amiga computer as its heart.

The CDTV player uses a hand-held control unit to control the on-screen cursor arrow or to interact with the program material. The player connects directly to a television set and can also be connected to a stereo system to enjoy the benefits of high fidelity stereophonic sound.

In addition to the proprietary-format CDTV discs, the player can also play audio CDs as well as CD+G discs.

OTHER FORMATS

There are several other proprietary CD-ROM formats that are intended exclusively for use with a particular machine. Many of these are recreational software products, such as those developed and produced for the TurboGraphics, Sega, and other CD-ROM game machines. These game machines are usually (but not always) also capable of playing audio CD's, and many include line-output jacks for connection to a stereo system in addition to a headphone jack.

Since these products are developed exclusively for use on their proprietary players, they are not inter-compatible with any other CD-ROM drive or consumer-level player.

REVIEW...

...All CD-ROM formats are not interchangeable.

...Compatibility is a major issue to consider when purchasing a consumer-level player for optical media.

...Kodak's Photo CDs can be single-session or multi-session.

...Not all computer CD-ROM drives can read Photo CDs, and some drives can read single-session but not multi-session discs.

...The interactivity level of consumer-level CD-ROM software is determined by the programming of the disc.

...All consumer-level players have a computer inside them, but user actions are limited by the hardware interface.

...Proprietary data formats usually can only be read by machines designed specifically for those formats.

Welcome To
CD
ROM
6

SELECTING A CD-ROM DRIVE

In this lesson...

…Internal and External Configurations

…Caddy-type and Caddyless drives

…Portable and Multidisc drives

…Drive and Software "Bundles"

…Mail Order Purchasing

...Additional terms and definitions

...Prices, specifications, and features of thirty-four popular CD-ROM drives

ALL CD-ROM DRIVES ARE NOT CREATED EQUAL

Just as there are different grades, makes, and models of automobiles for drivers with different tastes and budgets, CD-ROM drives, too, come in lots of different varieties.

One of the first issues you should settle before you begin shopping for a drive is the interfacing. If you're going to use the drive with a Macintosh or share it between a PC and a Mac you'll need a drive that has a SCSI interface. If you'll be using the drive exclusively with a PC, then either a proprietary or SCSI interface will suffice. However, the SCSI model is probably the best choice of these two types, all other factors being equal, since it allows daisychaining other SCSI devices and it is an industry-standard interface format.

As we also discussed in a previous lesson, CD-ROM drives are available in external and internal configurations. The external models are self-contained units that have their own power supplies and can easily be moved about from one place (or computer) to another. Internal CD-ROM drives, on the other hand, depend on the computer for power and are permanently mounted in a drive bay in the PC chassis, becoming an integral component of the computer itself.

With the increasing popularity of today's high-powered notebook and laptop computers, portable CD-ROM drives are also gaining in popularity with those who need (or want) to take their PC and optical media "on the road." Portable CD-ROM drives usually require plugging in an AC adapter to power the drive, although the NEC portable models also provide a rechargeable NiCad battery pack as an optional accessory for true portable operation. Portable drives usually use a parallel-to-SCSI adapter to interface with the laptop or notebook PC, since these machines rarely have an internal expansion slot to accommodate an interface card. Of course, a portable drive can also be used with a desktop PC or Macintosh as well. If you are a laptop or notebook computer user, you may want to seriously consider the merits of a portable CD-ROM drive, particularly if you anticipate doing some computing in different locations.

How the drive accepts and *mounts* the CD-ROM disc is also something to be considered, especially if you intend to build a CD-ROM library and will be changing discs in the drive often.

Many drives utilize a caddy to hold the disc. A caddy is a thin plastic and metal magazine that is hinged on its top side to permit CD-ROMs to be inserted or removed from it. With a CD-ROM loaded in the caddy, the caddy is then inserted into the CD-ROM drive. Caddies provide a convenient means of loading and unloading CD-ROMs from the drive without touching the disc itself, and they also offer additional protection for the media when it is not residing in its *jewel box*.

Some drives don't utilize a caddy at all. Instead, the CD-ROM is inserted directly into the drive mechanism. The two major types of caddyless drives utilize either a flip-up lid on the drive which provides access to the disc compartment or a drawer that slides out to receive the disc, just like many audio CD players. With caddyless drives, the CD-ROM itself is handled with each loading or unloading, since there is no caddy to hold or protect it.

The advantages of caddies are that they offer protection for the media and discs in caddies can be swapped faster. The down side is that caddies typically cost $10-$12 each, and require loading the disc into them before they can be used.

A **CADDY** is a thin plastic and metal magazine that is hinged on its top side to permit CD-ROMs to be inserted or removed from it. With a CD-ROM loaded in the caddy, the caddy is then inserted into the CD-ROM drive. Caddies provide a convenient means of loading and unloading CD-ROMs from the drive without touching the disc itself, and they also offer additional protection for the media.

A **JEWEL BOX** is the thin, almost-square hinged plastic case in which CD-ROMs and audio CDs come packed. In addition to protecting the disc during shipment, the jewel box also provides a place to store the disc when it is not in use in the drive or in a caddy, thus protecting it from dirt, scratches, and other foreign matter that could damage it or impair its readability.

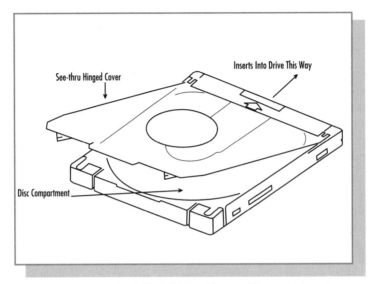

See-thru Hinged Cover

Inserts Into Drive This Way

Disc Compartment

FIGURE 6.1 *A standard CD-ROM caddy provides a quick and convenient way to change discs. The CD-ROM is held inside the disc compartment and protected by a hinged, see-thru cover. A sliding metal window on the bottom of the caddy permits access to the disc for the drive's rotation and reading mechanisms.*

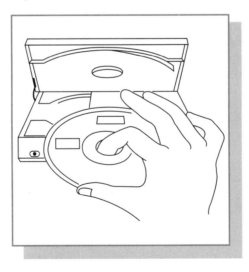

FIGURE 6.2 *A typical caddyless drive is illustrated above. The disc is inserted directly onto the drive spindle with this kind of drive, negating the need for a caddy. The excessive disc handling required is a major disadvantage of caddyless drives.*

Once loaded, however, the disc can remain in the caddy as its permanent home, ready for use instantly whenever desired. Having several caddies on hand significantly reduces the amount of physical disc handling required if frequent disc swapping is anticipated.

The advantage of a caddyless drive is that you are spared the expense of buying caddies, but as a trade-off you're giving up a certain element of protection and convenience inherent with a caddy. Caddyless drives also frequently (but not always) have slower access times than drives that use caddies.

ACCESS TIME is the time required for a CD-ROM drive to respond to a request for data, measured in milliseconds (thousandths of a second). The access time spans the elapsed time from the point the information request was made until the information is received. 350ms access time is considered about normal for the average CD ROM drive, with any access time lower than that being more desirable.

If your work entails using several CD-ROMs frequently you might want to consider a multi-disc drive or a *jukebox*. The Pioneer DRM-600A and the new multimedia-capable DRM-604X are both multi-disc drives that utilize a unique magazine approach to storing and serving discs. Similar in concept to a caddy, the Pioneer magazines contain six swing-out trays that each hold a single CD-ROM. The loaded magazine is inserted into the drive and six CD-ROMs become instantly accessible and on-line, ready for use whenever needed.

The jukebox approach provides a cabinet that can hold several daisy-chained individual CD-ROM drives all in one convenient enclosure. Since all of the drives contained in a jukebox are independent devices that all share a common controller, each drive can be accessed by its own unique device ID number. This makes the jukebox approach ideal for multi-user environments where several PCs are connected to the jukebox, as in a network. Under this scheme, multiple users can access different drives in the jukebox simultaneously. Conversely, the Pioneer multi-disc changers can only access one CD-ROM at a time, since there is only one drive mechanism. Of course, several Pioneer changers could also be daisychained to deliver enormous on-line CD-ROM resources.

In light of these physical variations for drive types, I'm frequently asked which configuration is the best. My answer is invariably *whatever configuration and price range works for you is best*. The most popular and flexible configuration is an external SCSI drive which uses a caddy for disc serv-

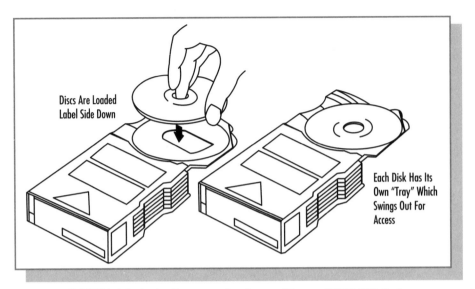

Discs Are Loaded
Label Side Down

Each Disk Has Its
Own "Tray" Which
Swings Out For
Access

FIGURE 6.3 A six-disc magazine from a Pioneer DRM-600 Series Multidisc CD-ROM changer is shown above. Unlike other drives or caddies which accept the CD-ROM(s) label-up, the Pioneer arrangement calls for label-side down loading in the magazine. Six CD-ROMs holding up to 3.2 gigabytes of data can be loaded simultaneously.

ing. This configuration permits moving the drive from one computer to another easily, doesn't require any particular technical skills to install, and it delivers the protection and benefits inherent with caddied disc serving.

Several performance-related factors come into play when selecting a CD-ROM drive, and these are more important than whether the drive is internal or external or uses a caddy or not. These performance issues deal with how fast the drive can find the information you desire on the disc (the access time), how quickly it can transfer the data to the PC once it is located (the sustained data-streaming rate), and how far "ahead" of the PC the drive can be working to provide a smooth and uninterrupted flow of data (the buffer size).

As is often the case with all types of computer hardware, the law of price versus performance applies to CD-ROM drives, too. It is a fact of life that the best and fastest drives are always more expensive than slower models. While there are many bargains to be had on low-priced drives that may be slightly older models left in stock, don't be too hasty in trying to save a few dollars. You may be penny wise but dollar foolish buying one of these drives, since it won't have the performance or buffering necessary for smooth full-motion video replay or other multimedia applications.

A **BUFFER** is a temporary holding area in memory where data is stored until an opportunity to complete its transfer arises. CD-ROM drives are equipped with built-in buffers that are used for data "streaming" or keeping a smooth and continuous flow of data coming at a constant rate of speed. The size of the buffer determines the sustained data transfer speed of the drive, with larger buffers (such as 64K) being preferable over smaller ones (typically 16K or 32K).

A few words about access time are in order here, and once again I'll use magnetic hard drives as a source of comparison. An access time of under 30ms (milliseconds) is considered average and acceptable for a hard drive on a PC, with any access time over 40ms thought to be excruciatingly slow. CD-ROM drives, in comparison then, must seem to be almost standing still with their average access times in the 300ms-350ms range. While 300ms is only three-tenths of a second, this can seem like an awfully long time when you're searching for some data on a CD-ROM as opposed to the same search on a hard drive. Access times have improved greatly for CD-ROM drives, however, from the 600ms-800ms times that were the norm just a few years ago, but they still have a long way to go before they approach the speedy performance of today's IDE magnetic hard drives.

IDE is an acronym for Integrated Drive Electronics, a design specification for magnetic hard disk drives that provides much of the drives' support and control circuitry built right into the drive itself rather than on a separate controller card.

EISA is an acronym for Extended Industry Standard Architecture, a bus standard that was introduced in 1988. EISA maintains backward compatibility with ISA (Industry Standard Architecture) in addition to adding many of the enhanced features IBM introduced with its Micro Channel Architecture bus standard including a 32-bit data path.

ISA is an acronym for Industry Standard Architecture, the widely accepted (but unofficial) designation for the bus design of the original IBM PC. The ISA specification was expanded to include a 16-bit data path in 1984 from its original 8-bit specification with the introduction of the IBM PC/AT computer.

MCA is an acronym for Micro Channel Architecture, the design of the bus used in IBM PS/2 computers (except for the Model 25 and Model 30). Micro Channel expansion slots are electrically and physically different from the standard IBM PC/AT (ISA) bus, so accessory or adapter cards for standard IBM-compatible PC's won't work in a Micro Channel machine.

OEM is an acronym for Original Equipment Manufacturer, this term is often used to describe hardware or software versions that are provided on a wholesale basis to other manufacturers who include the device or program in their final, finished product (such as a computer system).

SCSI-2 is an evolved SCSI standard as drafted by the American National Standards Institute that seeks to alleviate some of the compatibility problems sometimes encountered using SCSI devices by providing more stringent hardware design guidelines, additional device commands, better error handling and recovery, and enhanced logic for signal routing and device sharing. It is important to note that not all SCSI adapter cards can support newer devices that are built to conform to the SCSI-2 protocols.

BUNDLED DRIVE PACKAGES

Many of the major manufacturers frequently put together CD-ROM drive packages that come *bundled* with an interface kit and at least a few CD-

ROM software titles. With the swelling upsurge in the popularity of multimedia, some of the higher-end bundles also include a sound card, amplified speakers, and other audio accessories in addition to a high-speed multimedia-capable drive.

Bundles are usually terrific ways to get all of the elements required for CD-ROM all in one convenient package. As with any other computer equipment purchase, you should be an educated consumer and shop carefully, comparing features and value for several possible choices.

The major *caveat* to be observed when considering the purchase of a bundled package is that in many cases the super bargains are older products that no longer reflect the current state of the art. This applies to both the hardware and software portions of the bundle. For example, components of a "super starter package" might contain an older model drive with 700ms access time and a 16Kb buffer, along with some world almanac, encyclopedia, world atlas, shareware and public domain, and business statistic CD-ROM titles. This may be a terrific buy for the average PC user who can find hours of fascination exploring these gigabytes of information. For the person who wants to get the full benefits of multimedia, however, this bundle would be a disappointment since the drive isn't multimedia-capable nor are any of the software titles. And, while the vast majority of the data contained on these CD-ROMs are certainly still viable and accurate, since these discs are somewhat dated, the information won't be as complete as the current editions of these same discs, which are updated on a yearly basis in most cases.

Knowing what you're looking for and what your realistic budget considerations are will enable you to select a bundle that's going to be right for you now as well as a few months down the line.

Here are some examples of bundle offers that are available as of this writing. Since bundle packages are usually only available for a short time during the offer, these package combinations and prices probably won't apply by the time you read this, but they should serve well to give you an idea of what typical packages consist of.

Apple Computer put a bundle package together for its CD 300 CD-ROM drive. The dual-speed drive is available in either internal or external versions and comes bundled with a selection of software titles including a *Photo CD Sampler, Mozart: String Quartet in C Major and Cinderella* as well as several other titles. QuickTime software as well as the CD Access desk accessory and other utility software is also provided in the bundle. The SCSI drive plugs directly into any Macintosh's SCSI port.

The internal version carries a $499 suggested list, while the external version lists at $599.

NEC is currently offering two bundle specials: CD Express and Multimedia Gallery for both PC and Macintosh platforms.

CD Express retails for $499 and contains the MPC-compliant NEC CDR-25 CD-ROM drive, a PC or Macintosh interface kit, speakers, batteries and ten software titles including *Interactive Storytime, Lucasfilm Games, Reference Library* and others.

Multimedia Gallery retails for $999 and includes the CDR-74 CD-ROM drive, an audio board (PC version only), self-amplified stereo speakers, batteries, headphones, a microphone and six software titles including *The New Grolier Multimedia Encyclopedia, Great Wonders of the World, The Guinness Disc of World Records 1992* and others.

Sony is also providing a couple of bundle packages built around its CDU31A (internal) and CDU7305 (external) drives. These bundles are collectively called the *Sony Desktop Library.*

The CDU31A-LL/L bundle is a complete multimedia CD-ROM system including the internal version of the Sony drive, speakers, a sound board, *GeoWorks CD-ROM Manager, Tempra Access* Photo CD software and five multimedia titles: *The New Grolier Multimedia Encyclopedia, Great Wonders of the World Volume I, Where in the World is Carmen Sandiego?* (Deluxe Version), *The Presidents: It All Started with George,* and *The 1991 TIME Magazine Compact Almanac.* This bundle carries a suggested list price of $849.95.

The CDU7305 bundle has the exact same contents as the bundle above, except that the external version of the Sony drive is substituted along with the required external cabling. The price of this package is $1,069.95.

Sony also has an inexpensive starter-kit bundle that is designated as the CDU31A-LL/N. This bundle includes the internal Sony drive, *GeoWorks CD-ROM Manager, Tempra Access* Photo CD software and two multimedia titles: *The New Grolier Encyclopedia* and *Great Wonders of the World Volume I.* The suggested list price for this bundle is $499.95.

Damark, DAK, C.O.M.B., and other mail-order catalog houses also frequently offer bundle packages consisting of the drive, interface kit, and selected CD-ROM software titles, usually at very good prices. Be sure to do your homework before making a purchase, and you'll find that the time you invest in comparing prices for the same product from different sources can result in a substantial cash savings, although there are some precautions that apply to purchasing CD-ROM drives and related products via mail order that are addressed in the next section.

A **BRIDGE DISC** is a disc that plays on a CD-XA drive or a CD-I drive. The difference is that a low-level XA disc stores a table of contents, permitting you to view the tracks when used with an audio drive. CD-I does not—it changes at each sector and there's no TOC with a CD-I disc. A bridge disc's low-level format allows it to be played on both XA or CD-I players. An example of a bridge disc is the Kodak Photo CD.

HFS is an abbreviation for Hierarchical File System, a tree-structured file system on the Apple Macintosh in which folders can be "nested" within other folders. Early versions of the Macintosh operating systems (known as MFS, for Macintosh File System) supported only a flat-file system with no folders or subdirectories.

ISO 9660 is an international standard format for CD-ROM adopted by the International Organization for Standardization. This is the "legal" name for the High Sierra draft standard of the specification, with some modifications and enhancements.

HIGH SIERRA is an industry-wide drafted format specification for CD-ROM which defines the logical structure, file structure and record structures of a CD-ROM disc. It served as the basis for the ISO 9660, the formal international format standard for CD-ROM. High Sierra was named for the location of a meeting for CD-ROM industry representatives held near Lake Tahoe in November, 1985 where the standard was drafted.

HYBRID DISC is a CD-ROM that contains data written in two formats, HFS and ISO 9660, thus enabling the disc to be read and used by a Macintosh or an IBM-compatible PC.

DEFINITION

MAIL-ORDER PURCHASING

The same rules-of-thumb apply when purchasing a drive or bundled package via a mail order or catalog house. Knowing exactly what you're looking for is the most important element in purchasing any computer equipment via mail order, since you don't have the benefit of an in-person salesman to explain the differences between brands or models and present the various features and benefits of each. When perusing mail order advertisements, pay specific attention to the drive's specifications (such as access time, interfacing, and buffer size) and to the other components included or not included (such as interface, cables, and caddy). Some unscrupulous mail order houses advertise a drive at an astonishingly low price, then charge full list for all of the other components you'll need. Sometimes the total for these individual elements far exceeds what your local computer dealer charges for a name-brand bundled package, so be sure to be a wise shopper.

Read the fine print on any items you're thinking of purchasing via a mail order catalog, especially "close-out" specials. Some mail order catalog houses regularly handle "factory refurbished" equipment and offer it for sale at substantial savings. The terms "factory refurbished," "factory serviced," and "factory reconditioned" all mean one thing: there was something wrong with the unit the way it was originally sold and the customer returned it to the store. The store then returned it to the manufacturer who (hopefully) fixed it and then sold it to the catalog mail order house at a drastically-reduced price. Buying this kind of merchandise, even though it is still usually fully covered by the manufacturer's warranty, isn't prudent when it comes to delicate devices like computer systems and CD-ROM drives. Be sure that the merchandise you order is factory new, and not reconditioned, to avoid problems.

If you do decide to purchase from a mail order house, be certain you understand what their return and refund policies are for defective merchandise or if, for some reason, you just aren't happy with the products or their performance. Again, an ounce of prevention here in the way of asking questions is worth more than a pound of cure in the event that the merchandise doesn't turn out to be all you expected it to be.

Here, then, is a listing of the CD-ROM drives available as of this writing. I've made every attempt to make this listing as complete as possible, but with new drives models being released continuously, it may not include everything available by the time you read this. For precisely that reason I've also included a listing of the manufacturers' addresses and telephone numbers so you can contact them directly to obtain information on any new models that may have been released in the interim.

MANUFACTURER: APPLE COMPUTER, INC.

Drive Model:	CD-150
Configuration:	External
Interface:	SCSI
Access Time:	380ms (average)
Streaming Rate:	150Kb/sec (mode 1), 171Kb/sec (mode 2)
Capacity:	656Mb (mode 1), 748Mb (mode 2)
Price:	$499
Features:	A stand-alone drive with SCSI interface developed especially for all Macintosh Plus and above computers. The drive supports both the ISO 9660 and the High Sierra formats and can also read single-session Kodak Photo CD discs. Audio CD playback is supported through the drive's headphone or RCA jack, and the drive is supplied with an upgraded CD Remote desk accessory that allows the user to control volume directly from the computer.

MANUFACTURER: APPLE COMPUTER, INC.

Drive Model:	CD-300
Configuration:	External
Interface:	SCSI
Access Time:	360ms (average)
Streaming Rate:	150Kb/sec (mode 1), 171Kb/sec (mode 2)
Capacity:	656Mb (mode 1), 748Mb (mode 2)
Price:	$599
Features:	This is the new high-performance external SCSI drive from Apple designed specifically for multimedia uses on Macintosh computers or any PC with a SCSI interface. The CD-300 has a drive motor that spins twice as fast as ordinary drives, which results in faster access and continuous data streaming at the higher speeds required for today's demanding multimedia applications.

MANUFACTURER: CD TECHNOLOGY, INC.

Drive Model:	CD Porta-Drive T3301
Configuration:	External/Portable
Interface:	SCSI
Access Time:	200ms
Streaming Rate:	350Kb/sec
Capacity:	680Mb
Price:	$850
Features:	This drives weighs under four pounds and is compatible with any IBM PS/2, IBM PC, XT, AT, 386, 486, portable, and Apple Macintosh. It can also play audio CDs and has built-in dual RCA phone jacks along with a 64K memory buffer. Supports both 120v and 220v with automatic voltage switching. An optional carrying pouch is also available for taking it on the road with you.

MANUFACTURER: CD TECHNOLOGY, INC.

Drive Model:	CD Porta-Drive T3401-INT
Configuration:	Internal
Interface:	SCSI
Access Time:	200ms
Streaming Rate:	350Kb/sec
Capacity:	680Mb
Price:	$650
Features:	An internal drive for PCs and compatibles, it is supplied with a flat cable for daischaining three drives (internally). PlayCD software is included and this drive plays stereo audio through twin RCA jacks or its built-in headphone jack. It can also be used for multimedia uses.

MANUFACTURER: CHINON INDUSTRIES, INC.

Drive Model:	CDA-431
Configuration:	External
Interface:	SCSI
Access Time:	350ms
Streaming Rate:	150Kb/sec (continuous)
Capacity:	680Mb
Price:	$795

Features: An external drive that is compatible with Macintosh Plus, Macintosh SE/30, and Macintosh II series computers as well as IBM-compatible PCs. It reads Macintosh HFS, ISO 9660, and High Sierra format discs, and automatically recognizes ROM, audio and mixed audio/ROM discs. The CDA-431 comes standard with RCA jacks, SCSI interface cabling, and device-driver software and is bundled with Educorp's Shareware software. The drive features an audio volume knob, easy-access dip switches, and one-touch auto-eject button.

MANUFACTURER: CHINON INDUSTRIES, INC.

Drive Model:	CDS-431
Configuration:	Internal drive
Interface:	SCSI
Access Time:	350ms
Streaming Rate:	150Kb/sec (continuous)
Capacity:	680Mb
Price:	$650

Features: CDS-431, Chinon's internal IBM/PC and Apple Macintosh compatible CD-ROM drive is designed for OEM (original equipment manufacturers) applications. It occupies a standard half-height slot in IBM/PCs and comes complete with CD-ROM extensions software, interface card and cabling kit.

MANUFACTURER: CHINON INDUSTRIES, INC.

Drive Model:	CDX-431
Configuration:	External
Interface:	SCSI
Access Time:	350ms
Streaming Rate:	150Kb/sec (continuous)
Capacity:	680Mb
Price:	$650

Features: The CDX-431 is Chinon's external IBM/PC compatible CD-ROM/Audio Drive. This drive ships complete with SCSI connector, interface card, cabling kit, and Microsoft's MS-DOS Extensions software. As with other Chinon drives, the model CDX-431 automatically recognizes either ROM, audio or mixed audio/ROM discs.

MANUFACTURER: DENON AMERICA, INC.

Drive Model:	DRD-253
Configuration:	External

Interface:	SCSI
Access Time:	400ms (average)
Streaming Rate:	153 Kb/sec
Capacity:	680Mb
Price:	$1,100 (host adapter and cable included)
Features:	An imbedded SCSI controller is built-into all Denon drives. The DRD-253 is the self-powered stand alone version and it comes supplied with the SCSI adapter card, extensions software, and a disc caddy.

MANUFACTURER: HITACHI NEW MEDIA

Drive Model:	CDR 1750S MAC (CD-MAC2)
Configuration:	External
Interface:	SCSI
Access Time:	320ms (average)
Streaming Rate:	153.6 Kb/sec
Capacity:	682Mb (mode 1), 777.9 Mb (mode 2)
Price:	$995
Features:	This is an external drive that features a new error-correcting LSI chip, a 64Kb multi-function buffer, linear motor, audio capacity, three way caddy ejection, and daisychaining of up to eight units. An airtight chassis, dustproof double doors and an automatic pick-up lens cleaning (ALC) mechanism all contribute to the drive's reliability.

MANUFACTURER: HITACHI NEW MEDIA

Drive Model:	CDR-1700S
Configuration:	External
Interface:	Proprietary
Access Time:	320ms (average)
Streaming Rate:	153.6 Kb/sec
Capacity:	682Mb (mode 1), 777.9 Mb (mode 2)
Price:	$815
Features:	This model uses the Hitachi bus for interfacing rather than SCSI. The interface card is available for either the standard AT (ISA) or PS/2 (MCA) bus. This drive features a new error-correcting LSI chip, 32Kb multi-function buffer, linear motor, audio capacity, three way caddy ejection, and daisychaining of up to eight units.

MANUFACTURER: HITACHI NEW MEDIA

Drive Model:	CDR-1750s
Configuration:	External drive
Interface:	SCSI
Access Time:	320ms (average)
Streaming Rate:	153.6Kb/sec (mode 1), 175.2Kb/sec (mode 2)
Capacity:	682Mb (mode 1), 777.9Mb (mode 2)
Price:	$915 (drive only)
Features:	This is an external drive with SCSI interface that features Hitachi's new error-correcting LSI chip, 64Kb multifunction buffer, linear motor, audio capacity, and daisychaining of up to eight units. The drive can also be used as a boot device.

MANUFACTURER: HITACHI NEW MEDIA

Drive Model:	CDR-3700s
Configuration:	Internal
Interface:	Proprietary
Access Time:	300ms (average)
Streaming Rate:	153.6Kb/sec (mode 1), 175.2Kb/sec (mode 2)
Capacity:	682Mb (mode 1), 777.9Mb (mode 2)
Price:	$745 (drive only)
Features:	Another internal drive using Hitachi's proprietary interface card for the AT bus. In addition to the error-correcting LSI chip, 64Kb buffer, linear motor, 2 channel audio output with stepless volume control and daisychaining of up to eight units, this model also features an enhanced look-ahead cache memory. It comes complete with interface card, cable and MS-DOS CD-ROM Extensions and is suitable for multimedia applications.

MANUFACTURER: HITACHI NEW MEDIA

Drive Model:	CDR-3750s
Configuration:	Internal
Interface:	SCSI
Access Time:	300ms (average)
Streaming Rate:	153.6Kb/sec (mode 1), 175.2Kb/sec (mode 2)
Capacity:	682Mb (mode 1), 777.9Mb (mode 2)

Price: $865 (drive only)

Features: This is the fastest performing Hitachi internal drive with SCSI interface. It features a new error correcting LSI chip, 64Kb buffer, linear motor, two-channel audio output with stepless volume control, and daisychaining of up to eight units. Reliability is improved by an automatic pickup lens cleaning mechanism (ALC), a special double-door mechanism and an airtight chassis. It may be mounted vertically or horizontally. A SCSI card is also available. SCSI-2 commands are supported and the drive is suitable for multimedia applications.

MANUFACTURER: IBM CORPORATION

Drive Model:	PS/2 External CD-ROM Drive
Configuration:	External
Interface:	SCSI
Access Time:	380ms (average)
Streaming Rate:	150Kb/sec (sustained), 1.5Mb/sec (burst)
Capacity:	600Mb
Price:	$1,550

Features: This is a stand-alone external drive that attaches to the PS/2 system via a SCSI interface. The external version is for all Micro Channel PS/2s and it has audio output as well as daisychaining capability.

MANUFACTURER: IBM CORPORATION

Drive Model:	PS/2 Internal CD-ROM Drive
Configuration:	Internal
Interface:	SCSI
Access Time:	380ms (average)
Streaming Rate:	150Kb/sec (sustained), 1.5Mb/sec (burst)
Capacity:	600Mb
Price:	$1,550

Features: Essentially the same drive as its external counterpart, this internally-mounted model is intended for all Micro Channel PS/2 machines. Audio output and daisychaining capability is supported.

MANUFACTURER: NEC TECHNOLOGIES (USA), INC.

Drive Model:	CDR-35
Configuration:	External/Portable

Interface:	SCSI
Access Time:	500ms (average)
Streaming Rate:	150Kb/sec (sustained), 1.5Mb/sec (burst)
Capacity:	540Mb (DOS), 540Mb (Apple)
Price:	$599
Features:	This is a stand-alone drive that becomes portable with the optional battery pack. It is compatible with Macintosh, IBM PC/XT/AT, PS/2, and 100-percent IBM compatibles. Light and compact, it is ideal for use with laptop or notebook PCs and has audio output.

MANUFACTURER: NEC TECHNOLOGIES (USA), INC.

Drive Model:	CDR-36
Configuration:	External/Portable
Interface:	SCSI
Access Time:	500ms (average)
Streaming Rate:	150Kb/sec (sustained), 1.5Mb/sec (burst)
Capacity:	540Mb (DOS), 680Mb (Apple)
Price:	$599
Features	Adding the optional NiCad battery pack makes this drive a portable unit that is compatible with Macintosh, PC-compatibles and PS/2 machines. Audio output is supported through a headphone jack with thumbwheel volume control.

MANUFACTURER: NEC TECHNOLOGIES (USA), INC.

Drive Model:	CDR-37
Configuration:	External/Portable
Interface:	SCSI
Access Time:	450ms (average)
Streaming Rate:	150Kb/sec (sustained), 1.5Mb/sec (burst)
Capacity:	680Mb
Price:	$599
Features:	Another portable CD-ROM drive that can utilize a NiCad battery pack, this model features user-selectable device IDs of 0 through 7 and is compatible with Macintosh, PC-compatibles and PS/2 machines. The drive weighs only 2.2 pounds by itself and only 3 pounds with the battery pack attached.

MANUFACTURER: NEC TECHNOLOGIES (USA), INC.

Drive Model:	CDR-36M
Configuration:	External/Portable (MPC)
Interface:	SCSI
Access Time:	450ms (average)
Streaming Rate:	150Kb/sec (sustained), 1.5Mb/sec (burst)
Price:	$549
Features:	This is NEC's MPC-compatible stand alone drive that becomes portable with the optional battery pack. Compatible with Macintosh, IBM PC/XT/AT, PS/2 and 100-percent IBM compatibles, the drive also features a headphone jack with volume control for audio output.

MANUFACTURER: NEC TECHNOLOGIES (USA), INC.

Drive Model:	CDR-73
Configuration:	External drive
Interface:	SCSI
Access Time:	300ms (average)
Streaming Rate:	150Kb/sec (sustained), 1.5Mb/sec (burst)
Capacity:	540Mb (DOS), 680Mb (Apple)
Price:	$899 (drive only)
Features:	An external, stand-alone drive that is compatible with Macintosh, IBM XT/AT, PS/2, and 100-percent IBM compatibles. Audio output is supported through a headphone jack with volume control and dual (right and left channel) RCA jacks. This drive can be used vertically or horizontally.

MANUFACTURER: NEC TECHNOLOGIES (USA), INC.

Drive Model:	CDR-73M
Configuration:	External drive (MPC)
Interface:	SCSI
Access Time:	280ms (average)
Streaming Rate:	300Kb/sec (sustained), 1.5Mb/sec (burst)
Capacity:	540Mb (DOS), 680Mb (Apple)
Price:	$899
Features:	This is the MPC-compatible version of the CDR-72. Like the 73, the 73M is an external drive for Macs, PCs and PS/2 machines using a SCSI interface. Vertical or horizontal operation is supported, as is audio output.

MANUFACTURER: NEC TECHNOLOGIES (USA), INC.

Drive Model:	CDR-83
Configuration:	Internal drive
Interface:	SCSI
Access Time:	300ms (average)
Streaming Rate:	150Kb/sec (sustained), 1.5Mb/sec (burst)
Capacity:	540Mb (DOS), 680Mb (Apple)
Price:	$799
Features:	A half-height internal drive that utilizes a SCSI interface. The drive ships with a flat SCSI ribbon cable and a disc caddy. The interface and driver software is not included and must be purchased separately for Macintosh, PC-compatibles and PS/2 computers.

MANUFACTURER: NEC TECHNOLOGIES (USA), INC.

Drive Model:	CDR-83M
Configuration:	Internal(MPC)
Interface:	SCSI
Access Time:	300ms (average)
Streaming Rate:	300Kb/sec (sustained), 1.5Mb/sec (burst)
Capacity:	540Mb (DOS), 560Mb (Apple)
Price:	$799
Features:	This is the internal MPC-compatible version of the CDR-83 that is also compatible with Macintosh, IBM PC/XT/AT, PS/2 and 100-percent IBM compatibles. Utilizing NECs MultiSpin technology, this drive is well-suited for demanding multimedia applications.

MANUFACTURER: PANASONIC COMMUNICATIONS

Drive Model:	LK-MC501S
Configuration:	External
Interface:	SCSI
Access Time:	500ms (average)
Streaming Rate:	153Kb/sec (sustained), 1.3Mb/sec (burst)
Capacity:	540Mb
Price:	$849 (drive only)
Features:	This is an external drive that uses SCSI interfacing. The LK-MC501S is compatible with both Macintosh and IBM-compatible PCs. This drive is also capable of running multimedia applications as well as playing audio CDs.

MANUFACTURER: PANASONIC COMMUNICATIONS

Drive Model:	LK-MC501B
Configuration:	Internal
Interface:	SCSI
Access Time:	500ms (average)
Streaming Rate:	153Kb/sec (sustained), 1.3Mb/sec (burst)
Capacity:	540Mb
Price:	$619 (drive only)
Features:	This drive is the internal counterpart of the Panasonic LK-MC501S and it uses SCSI interfacing. Compatible with both Macintosh and IBM-compatible PCs, this drive is also capable of running multimedia applications as well as playing audio CDs.

MANUFACTURER: PHILIPS INTERACTIVE MEDIA SYSTEMS (PIMS)

Drive Model:	CM 205
Configuration:	Internal (MPC)
Interface:	Proprietary
Access Time:	375ms (average)
Streaming Rate:	153.6Kb/sec (mode 1)
Capacity:	600Mb
Price:	$499
Features:	The CM 205 CD-ROM features fast access time and an intelligent buffer/cache. Designed for IBM XT/AT-compatible PCs, the CM 205 is compatible with the latest Multimedia PC (MPC) requirements.

MANUFACTURER: PIONEER COMMUNICATIONS

Drive Model:	DRM-600A
Configuration:	External/Multichanger
Interface:	SCSI
Access Time:	600ms (average)
Streaming Rate:	153Kb/sec (sustained), 1.5Mb/sec (burst)
Capacity:	3.2Gb (540Mb/disc)
Price:	$1,195

Features: The CD-ROM Changer is a stand alone drive with SCSI interface that can hold up to 6 CD discs and can daisychain up to seven units. Audio output is supported through headphone and RCA jacks, and it can also play standard CD Audio discs. This drive works with Macintosh, PC-compatible, and PS/2 machines.

MANUFACTURER: PIONEER COMMUNICATIONS

Drive Model:	DRM-604X
Configuration:	External
Interface:	SCSI
Access Time:	300ms
Streaming Rate:	612/153 Kb/sec (3.0Mb/sec burst)
Capacity:	3.2Gb (540Mb/disc)
Price:	$1,795

Features   This is the multimedia-capable version of the venerable DRM-600A multichanger. The disc rotates at four times the normal speed in this drive, achieving a phenomenal 612Kb-per-second data-transfer rate with standard CD-ROM discs. New VLSI chips, optical head, and loading mechanisms were developed to achieve rotational speeds up to 2,100 RPM, and the drive is equipped with a 128Kb data buffer for demanding multimedia applications. This drive also supports the SCSI-2 command set for CD-ROM devices and is capable of playing standard audio compact discs via its headphone or RCA jacks.

MANUFACTURER: PROCOM TECHNOLOGY, INC.

Drive Model:	MCD-ROM 650/M
Configuration:	External
Interface:	SCSI
Access Time:	325ms
Streaming Rate:	150Kb/sec (sustained) (5Mb/sec burst)
Capacity:	650 Mb
Price:	$859

Features: An external Macintosh and PC-compatible drive, it features an external SCSI I.D. dial for easy installation and setup of the device ID. Audio CD playback capability is included and a stereo headphone jack is provided.

MANUFACTURER: SONY CORPORATION

Drive Model:	CDU-535
Configuration:	Internal
Interface:	Proprietary
Access Time:	340ms (average)
Streaming Rate:	150Kb/sec (sustained), 1.5Mb/sec (burst)
Price:	$429.95 (drive only)
Features	This is a half-height internal drive with proprietary Sony bus interfacing and built-in audio headphone circuitry. Up to seven units can be daisychained.

MANUFACTURER: SONY CORPORATION

Drive Model:	CDU-541
Configuration:	Internal
Interface:	SCSI
Access Time:	380ms (average)
Streaming Rate:	150Kb/sec (sustained), 1.5Mb/sec (burst)
Price:	$699.95
Features:	Another half-height internal drive with SCSI interface and built-in audio headphone circuitry from Sony that can daisychain up to seven units and supports SCSI-2 commands.

MANUFACTURER: SONY CORPORATION

Drive Model:	CDU-31A
Configuration:	External drive
Interface:	Proprietary
Access Time:	550ms (average)
Streaming Rate:	150Kb/sec (sustained), 600Kb/sec (burst)
Price:	$378.00
Features	This external drive is a stand-alone unit that utilizes the proprietary Sony 40-pin bus connector. Audio line output is also supported, and up to four units can be daisychained. The drive features a 64Kb buffer to run multimedia applications smoothly.

MANUFACTURER: SONY CORPORATION

Drive Model:	CDU-7211
Configuration:	External

Interface:	SCSI
Access Time:	380ms (average)
Streaming Rate:	150Kb/sec (sustained), 1.2Mb/sec (burst)
Price:	$919.95
Features:	Another external Sony stand-alone drive, this model utilizes SCSI interfacing and is Kodak Photo CD multisession compatible. SCSI-2 commands are recognized and up to seven drives can be daisychained. Audio CD playback is also supported.

MANUFACTURER: RADIO SHACK

Drive Model:	Tandy CDR-1000
Configuration:	Internal
Interface:	Proprietary
Access Time:	375ms (average)
Streaming Rate:	150Kb/sec
Price:	$399.95
Features:	This internal CD-ROM drive comes complete with interface adapter, CD-ROM driver software, CD player software, and all necessary cables. This drive eliminates the caddy by using a front-serving tray loading system similar to an audio CD player.

REVIEW...

...Access times, buffer sizes, and data streaming rates vary greatly from drive to drive.

...Performance and features affect the price of a CD-ROM drive.

...Internal/external configuration, SCSI or proprietary.

...Interfacing, caddy-type, or caddyless disc serving are all important points to consider when purchasing a drive.

...External drives with SCSI interfaces are the most popular and flexible configurations.

...An external SCSI drive can be used with Macintosh and PC-compatible computers.

...Bundled packages frequently provide an economical way of getting everything you need to get started in CD-ROM.

...Knowing exactly what you want and how much you're willing to spend simplifies selecting a drive or bundle package.

...Older drive models and older CD-ROM software products are frequently bundled together in mail-order catalogs and can represent terrific bargains.

Welcome To

CD ROM

7

INSTALLING, CONFIGURING, AND USING A CD-ROM DRIVE

In this lesson...

…What's required for an installation

…General precautions for safety

…Macintosh external drive installation and setup

…IBM PS/2 external drive installation and setup

…PC Laptop/Notebook external installation and setup

…PC internal drive installation and setup

...PC external drive installation and setup

...Installing device drivers and extensions software

Installing a CD-ROM drive is a fairly straight-forward and relatively uncomplicated procedure that can be performed by virtually any user who's willing to invest some time and follow some very basic directions.

This lesson is divided into sections that deal with the specific installation procedures for the different computer configurations listed above, so you'll find the specific information on installing a drive with your computer in the appropriate section. I most heartily recommend that you read through *all* of the different installations and study the photos, since it gives you a more in-depth understanding of how installations on different hardware types share similarities but have some important differences as well.

All of the installation scenarios covered here are focused on SCSI-interfaced CD-ROM drives. The installation for a proprietary-interfaced drive is virtually identical except that a proprietary interface card replaces the SCSI card. The cable attachment for both internal and external installations is the same as for a SCSI installation, and the software installation is the same as well except that the SCSI driver is replaced with a proprietary one. If you're installing a proprietary-interface drive, follow the corresponding SCSI installation scenario (internal or external) with the appropriate proprietary substitutions and you shouldn't have any problems.

Even though the installation procedures vary somewhat depending on the computer, interface and drive, there are several common elements that apply to all installations. Here's a quick checklist of the items that are required for any CD-ROM installation:

1. a screwdriver (or two)
2. a host PC
3. an interface
4. a CD-ROM drive
5. a cable to connect items #3 and #4
6. a setup diskette containing the required software
7. a CD-ROM disc to check the functionality

If you have all of the above items, you're ready to start installing your CD-ROM drive. But first a few words about safety and general advice to make the installation go smoother.

SAFETY FIRST

Regardless of what computer you have—Macintosh, PC, or notebook—make absolutely sure the power cord is disconnected from the machine before you attempt any installation. On some Macs, PS/2, and PC machines it is also advisable to disconnect the monitor, keyboard, mouse, printer, modem, or any other cables that are connected to the machine, and remove these items to a safe location so you can have free and unobstructed access to the rear of the machine.

Having a clean, well-lit work area is also a good idea, as is thoroughly reading through all of the supplied instructions that came with the drive and interface kit to make sure you know exactly what is involved. Make a note of the manufacturer's tech support phone number as well as flagging the appropriate section on troubleshooting in the installation manual. This way, in the unlikely event that you run into a problem, you'll have the information you need to solve it right at hand.

STATIC ELECTRICITY

If your installation requires opening up the computer to insert an interface card, extra precautions are in order. Many of the components on the interface card as well as elsewhere inside the computer are very sensitive to static electricity. The same "shock" you get when touching a metal doorknob after walking across a carpeted room can wreak havoc to these delicate components.

To avoid problems, make sure you discharge yourself of any residual static electricity you may be carrying by touching a metal object such as the desk or a chair before touching any electronic components. As an extra precaution, avoid touching any of the components on the interface card or the metal "fingers" that insert into the expansion slot. Observing these precautions will prevent having any static electrical discharge problems during your installation.

TOOLS

Depending on the computer you're using for the installation, the only tools you'll need are a couple of screwdrivers. One should be a medium-sized flat blade or Phillips blade (depending on what type of screws your PC case cover is held on with), and a smaller screwdriver with a flat blade about one-eighth of an inch wide. This small screwdriver is used for securing the cable to the interface, a good practice to ensure it won't be pulled loose accidentally.

FIGURE 7.1 *Most installations only require either a Phillips or flat-blade screwdriver. A small blade screwdriver (sometimes called a jeweler's or precision screwdriver) is useful for tightening the small screws used to attach external connecting cables.*

If you experience a device conflict that requires changing a jumper cap on the interface card, you may find a pair of needle-nosed pliers or tweezers to be useful. In the majority of installations, however, the default configurations work without any modification.

INSTALLATION OVERVIEW

The sequence of events and procedures for every CD-ROM drive installation consists of:

1. installing the interface (not required on Macs)
2. connecting the drive to the interface

3. providing power for the drive

4. installing setup software to configure the system

Software installation is covered in detail following this pictorial section, which illustrates and describes CD-ROM drive installation on various hardware platforms.

MACINTOSH EXTERNAL CD-ROM DRIVE INSTALLATION

FIGURE 7.2 *All Macintosh Plus, SE, and II series computers have built-in SCSI interfaces. The SCSI ports are shown in the photo above, with a Mac LC II on the left and a Mac Classic II on the right.*

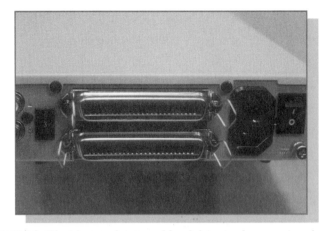

FIGURE 7.3 *The Macintosh internal hard drive is always assigned as device 0, so the device ID of the CD-ROM drive must be set to a non-conflicting ID number (1-7). The Apple CD 300 drive, shown above, permits changing the device ID number by using push-buttons to advance or decrease the device ID number setting. This is set to device #3.*

FIGURE 7.4 *Once the device ID is set, the SCSI cable can be attached to the first port on the drive. The opposite end of the cable is then attached to the SCSI port on the rear of the Mac, as shown above. The cable-securing screws should be tightened (the small blade screwdriver will come in handy here) to prevent the cable from becoming disconnected accidentally. When this step is completed, power cables can be reconnected to the Mac as well as the drive, along with the keyboard, printer and any other devices which were disconnected.*

FIGURE 7.5 *The Apple CD 150 and CD 300 models are both caddy-type drives. A disc is shown being inserted into a caddy, label-side up, prior to putting it into the Mac's new CD-ROM drive.*

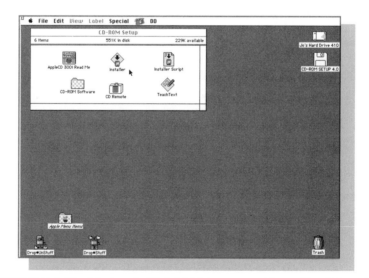

FIGURE 7.6 *The Macintosh CD-ROM drives come with a utility diskette that contains the programs and data required for the drive to work with the computer. Clicking on the installer icon starts the process, which involves copying files from the floppy diskette onto the Mac's hard disk in various locations like the system folder. When the process is completed, the Macintosh must be restarted for it to acknowledge the CD-ROM drive's presence.*

FIGURE 7.7 Multiple drives can be daisychained, as shown above, by simply giving each drive a unique device ID number. The CD 150 above (with the caddy being inserted) is assigned as device 1 while the CD 300 sitting on top of it is device 2. Up to seven devices can be connected through SCSI daisychaining.

IBM PS/2 External CD-ROM Drive Installation

FIGURE 7.8 Installing a SCSI interface card in an IBM PS/2 machine (a PS/2 Model 50Z is shown here) begins by loosening the two slotted thumb screws at the rear of the machine and lifting off the system cover. Be sure to unplug all cables first.

FIGURE 7.9 *A Trantor T-228 SCSI adapter card designed for MCA (Micro Channel Architecture) machines like the PS/2 50Z is shown above. The spring-held blocking plates should be removed from the expansion slot that is to receive the interface card. A slight tug is all that is required to remove the plate.*

FIGURE 7.10 *Align the "fingers" at the bottom of the interface card with the channel in the middle of the expansion slot and press downward with a firm, even pressure at the front and back of the board until you feel it "seated" in the slot. When properly seated the metal mounting bracket is flushly-aligned with the opening for it at the rear of the PC with no visible gaps. Once the card is installed the PS/2 system unit cover can be replaced.*

FIGURE 7.11 *With the system cover back in place and secured with the thumb screws, the SCSI connecting cable can now be attached to the SCSI port on the newly-installed adapter card. Tighten the screws of the connector cable using the small-bit screwdriver for the best contact and also to prevent accidental disconnection. All other cables, including the power cable and monitor, can now be reattached to the PS/2.*

FIGURE 7.12 *The drive shown above has a terminator installed in its second (lower) SCSI port, while the cable coming from the PS/2 mates with the drive's first SCSI port. Depending on the drive and SCSI interface adapter used, a terminator plug may be required for proper communication between the host PC and the drive. The terminator merely tells the host PC "this is the end of the line—there are no more devices after me," and isn't always required since some SCSI cards are pre-terminated for a single device.*

FIGURE 7.13 *The IBM PS/2 Reference Diskette (right) above is required to "tell" the system that a new card (the SCSI adapter) has been added, and this involves making a working copy of the Reference Diskette (see the PS/2 manual for details). Once this is accomplished, the installation of software drivers and any other required files including the Microsoft CD-ROM extensions can be performed using the utility diskette supplied with the drive and/or SCSI adapter card.*

PC Laptop/Notebook External Installation

FIGURE 7.14 *Unlike desktop PCs, laptop and notebook computers don't provide expansion slots to accommodate a SCSI adapter. A parallel-to-SCSI adapter solves this problem, however, by attaching directly to the PC's parallel printer port, as shown above. This NEC UltraLite SL/25C Notebook computer has a Trantor T-338 MiniSCSI adapter installed, with the SCSI cable attached to its opposite end going to the NEC CDR-37 portable CD-ROM drive next to it.*

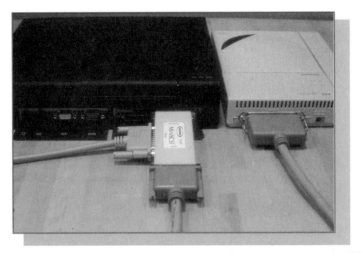

FIGURE 7.15 *The printer cable can be attached to a connector on the T-338 so printer functionality is maintained. When the T-338 isn't busy managing SCSI activity it is totally "transparent" to the port so printer operation is not affected in any way.*

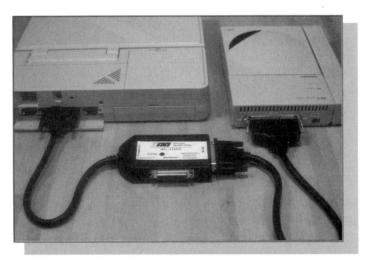

FIGURE 7.16 *The Always AL-1000 parallel-to-SCSI adapter is physically slightly larger than the Trantor unit, but provides some additional installation flexibility with its dual-cabled ends. As with the Trantor unit, the printer cable attaches to a middle connector making the device "transparent" when not in use and thus leaving normal printer functions unimpeded. The green LED on the AL-1000 is a handy feature that confirms a positive connection and power to the SCSI port.*

FIGURE 7.17 *With the parallel-to-SCSI adapter in place and the cable connecting it and the drive attached, all that remains is installing the required drivers and extensions using the automated install utility supplied with the adapter and/or drive. Parallel-to-SCSI adapters are ideal for use with notebooks as shown above by this CAF SuperLite 386SL/20 connected to an NEC CDR-36 portable CD-ROM drive. Note the external NiCad battery pack attached to the left side of the drive for truly portable operation without AC power.*

PC—INTERNAL CD-ROM DRIVE INSTALLATION

FIGURE 7.18 *Whether your PC is in a desktop case or a tower case, as shown in these photos, the same installation steps apply. To get started, first disconnect all power cables as well as any other cables (such as for your keyboard, mouse, modem, or printer) that may interfere with the installation. When all cables are disconnected, remove the screws that retain the case cover and remove the cover.*

FIGURE 7.19 *A half-height drive bay that is accessible from the front of the machine is required for mounting an internal CD-ROM drive. The uppermost bay in the photo above is where the NEC CDR-84 internal drive will nestle when installed.*

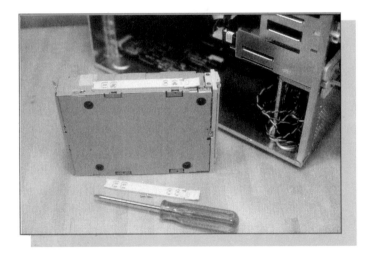

FIGURE 7.20 *Depending on the PC, you may have to install rails on the CD-ROM drive. Rails are plastic strips that, when secured to the drive by screws, ride in channels in the PC's case to support the drive. The photo above shows a rail being installed on the NEC drive, and these rails snap-lock into the channels in the case. On installations where rails are not used, the drive is secured to the case using the same screw holes used for mounting rails.*

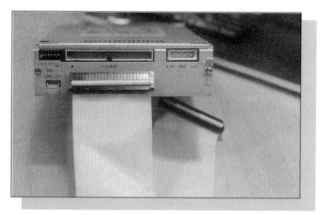

FIGURE 7.21 *A fifty-conductor ribbon cable is used to mate the CD-ROM drive with the internal pins of the interface. Orienting the cable with pin 1 on the drive and interface is of the utmost importance, since the drive won't work if the connection is reversed. The ribbon cable will have a "tracer" (a solid or dashed line in red, blue, white or some other contrasting color) on the "pin 1" side of the cable to facilitate correct orientation.*

FIGURE 7.22 *The cable connector on the drive also has some marking to let you know which is the pin 1 side as a guide for affixing the cable. Sometimes this marking is merely an arrow head pointing to pin 1, although the numerals "1" and "50" are used to identify the opposing ends of the pin rows. The drive shown above has its ribbon connector already attached prior to installing it in the bay. Attaching the ribbon cable first, as here, lessens the chance of bending a pin while trying to attach the cable after the drive is already in the bay.*

FIGURE 7.23 *The pigtail connector coming from the PC's power supply supplies the voltage for running the drive. In most installations, this connector can be attached after the drive is installed in the bay, but in really cramped cases it may be easier to feed the connector through the bay and attach it to the drive if there is enough slack in the cable to do so. The connector is "keyed" so it can only be inserted with the correct orientation.*

FIGURE 7.24 *The drive, with ribbon cable attached, is then slid into the bay in the PC chassis and secured. Some rails snap-lock into slots in the rail channels to secure the drive. Other cases may require securing the drive with screws or a retainer. Once the drive is seated and secured in the bay, the pigtail power connector can be attached if it is not already plugged into the drive.*

FIGURE 7.25 Locate pin 1 on the interface card to ensure proper orientation of the ribbon cable. The first pin position is identified on the card with either a numeric designation or some other identifier. Again, correct orientation of the ribbon cable is essential for the drive to work.

FIGURE 7.26 It is fairly easy to bend a pin when attaching the ribbon cable to the interface card, or to miss a row of pins completely. For these reasons it is advisable to attach the cable to the interface card before installing the card in the expansion slot if possible. Be sure the connector is aligned properly with all of the pins before pushing it all the way down on them.

FIGURE 7.27 *The interface card, with ribbon cable attached, can then be inserted into the expansion slot. Try to use an expansion slot for the adapter card that is as close to the drive as possible to avoid unnecessary "detours" around other cables or components inside the chassis. Once the card is fully seated in the expansion slot, it should be secured using the screw that formerly held the blocking plate for that slot in place.*

FIGURE 7.28 *Alternatively, you may also install the interface card before attaching the ribbon cable to the 50-pin connector on the card. Depending on the case design and how cramped the installation site is, it may be easier to install the card sans cable first. Be sure to avoid touching any of the components on the interface card to prevent any damage from static electricity.*

FIGURE 7.29 *If you're attaching the cable after the card is already installed in the slot, be extra careful to make sure you don't miss or bend any pins when attaching the cable connector. Of course, proper pin 1 orientation is also essential, so double-check the cable orientation and attachment to the pins on the adapter card.*

FIGURE 7.30 *When the card is fully seated in the expansion slot, it should be secured using the screw that formerly held the blocking plate for that slot in place. Securing the card can be done with or without the ribbon connector installed.*

FIGURE 7.31 *Putting the case cover back on the PC and reattaching all cables comes next. When that's finished, turn on the PC and proceed to install the required drivers and CD-ROM extension software supplied with the drive and/or interface kit.*

PC—EXTERNAL CD-ROM DRIVE INSTALLATION

FIGURE 7.32 *Disconnect all cables, remove all securing screws, and lift off the system cover, as with an internal PC drive installation. Once you have access to the expansion slots, select a convenient slot for the installation of the interface card and remove the backing plate for this slot. Be sure to avoid contact with the electronic components on the interface card to minimize the chance for any static charge damage to the interface.*

FIGURE 7.33 *Insert the adapter card in the selected expansion slot, pushing it in with firm, even pressure at both sides, until you feel it firmly "seat" itself in the slot.*

FIGURE 7.34 *Secure the interface card using the screw that formerly held the blocking plate for that expansion slot. At this point, the case cover can also be reinstalled on the PC and secured with its screws.*

FIGURE 7.35 *A terminator plug may be required in the drive's second SCSI port with some systems or configurations. The terminator plug can be inserted after the driver and extension software is installed if the drive doesn't respond as expected. Unless the manufacturer specifically advises otherwise in the installation manual, try the drive without a terminator plug in place first (it works without a terminator in the majority of installations).*

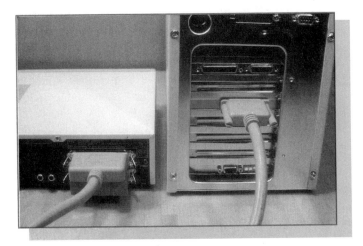

FIGURE 7.36 *Next the SCSI cable is attached to both the port on the interface card and to the CD-ROM drive. When these connections are made, all other cables including the power cables for both the PC and the CD-ROM drive can be installed.*

FIGURE 7.37 *Multiple drives can be daisychained through the SCSI ports, as shown above. Note that the terminator is inserted in the second SCSI port of the top drive, indicating that there are no other SCSI devices after this one connected to the adapter. Terminators are almost always required on the last device in a daisychain when more than one SCSI device is connected. Software installation of the required device drivers and Microsoft CD-ROM extensions completes the installation of this external CD-ROM drive on a PC.*

MACINTOSH SOFTWARE INSTALLATION

Installing the required operating system extension software, file handling utilities, and the desk accessory for playing audio CDs on the drive is blissfully simple on the Macintosh.

After attaching the connecting cable to both the Mac's SCSI port and the port on the drive, you can turn on the drive and then power-up the Macintosh as well, in that order.

Insert the CD-ROM installation diskette into the Mac's floppy drive and click on the installer icon with your mouse. Accept the defaults for file copies destinations and click on the continue box to commence the installation process. The installation program automatically copies the required files and puts them in the appropriate locations (system folder, extension folder, and so forth) depending on the Apple Operating System version you're running on your Mac. For Photo CD and QuickTime play capabilities, System 7.0 or later is required. If your operating system software is outdated the install program informs you of that and tells you what you need.

When completed, the Macintosh ejects the install floppy and reboots the computer for you. As the opening Mac screens come up, you'll see the CD-ROM identifier icon displayed at the bottom of the screen and an icon for the CD-ROM drive (or drives) are displayed under the icon for the Mac's hard drive.

At that point all you need do is insert a disc in the CD-ROM drive, click on the CD-ROM drive icon, then on the application's icon when it is displayed, and start enjoying the wondrous world of CD-ROM on your Macintosh.

PS/2 Software Installation

Installing the required drivers and operating system extension software on a PS/2 machine is the same as on a standard PC-compatible described in the next section, except that an extra step is required with a PS/2 machine.

IBM's PS/2 computers, such as the Model 50Z, require an update of the system's inventory whenever a peripheral device is physically added to the computer. A SCSI or proprietary CD-ROM interface card is such a peripheral.

Updating this peripheral device inventory is done via the IBM Reference Diskette that is supplied with your PS/2 machine. Follow the instructions in the Quick Reference guide supplied with your PC for instructions on how to make a copy of the original reference diskette and add the information from your interface's installation diskette.

When your work with the reference diskette is completed, the PS/2 machine will be "looking" for a new interface adapter the next time it is turned off and back on again. At this point you can eject the reference floppy diskette if it is still in the drive and shut the computer off.

Connect the CD-ROM drive via the SCSI cable if it isn't already attached, turn on the CD-ROM drive and then the PS/2 machine, in that order. The PS/2 should not display any error messages if the adapter card is properly inserted and the hardware table has been successfully updated.

You should now continue with the rest of the software installation described in the next section under PC installation.

PC SOFTWARE INSTALLATION

To access and retrieve information from a CD-ROM drive, it is necessary to install the Microsoft CD-ROM Extensions (MSCDEX.EXE) and appropriate device drivers into your computer's configuration file. The necessary software, extensions and drivers are provided with the installation disk that comes with the CD-ROM drive and/or interface kit, and once installed, requires no additional attention.

The purpose of these extensions and drivers is to allow the host computer to address and access the CD-ROM drive as though it is just another gigantic read-only hard drive. These extensions and drivers assign a logical identifier to the CD-ROM drive (such as device D or E), and permit you to "log" onto it as if it were a floppy or hard drive, list the directory, change sub-directories, copy files from it and perform other routine tasks.

An automated installation program is on the diskette that automatically copies over necessary files onto your hard drive and makes modifications to your AUTOEXEC.BAT and CONFIG.SYS files so that your system recognizes the CD-ROM drive.

Essentially, the automatic install program creates a subdirectory on your PC's hard disk (such as CDSYS) that holds the extension files and any other required setup software for the CD-ROM drive. The AUTOEXEC.BAT file is modified to include a couple of extra lines that set the path variable to include the CDSYS subdirectory, set the RAM allocation for buffer size and any other required parameters. The CONFIG.SYS file is also modified to add a LASTDRIVE line if required, insert a DEVICE line to acknowledge presence of the CD-ROM drivers and set the required parameters for it. Typical AUTOEXEC.BAT and CONFIG.SYS file listings are shown below as examples.

EXAMPLE AUTOEXEC.BAT CONTENTS:

```
@ECHO OFF
PROMPT $p $g
C:\CDSYS\MSCDEX /D:MSCD001 /M:8
PATH C:\DOS;C:\CDSYS;
```

EXAMPLE OF CONFIG.SYS CONTENTS:

```
LASTDRIVE=Z
FILES=30
BUFFERS=20
DEVICE=C:\DOS\HIMEM.SYS
DEVICE=C:\CDSYS\CDROMCRV.SYS /D:MSCD001 /U:1 /M:10
```

When the install program is finished with the copying and modifying the required files, remove the floppy diskette, and turn the PC off. Then turn on the CD-ROM drive, insert a disc, power-on the PC and start using and enjoying your new CD-ROM drive.

REVIEW...

...All power cables should be disconnected from the computer before an installation is performed.

...Regardless of the hardware requirements for installation, software installation is also a necessary element.

...Alignment of the first pin with the proper end of a ribbon connector is crucial for proper drive operation.

...Drives may not always require a terminator if used singly.

...Daisychained CD-ROM drives usually require a terminator on the last device in the chain.

...PS/2 machines require an update of the machine's hardware inventory, which is done via the PS/2 Reference Diskette.

...Installing a CD-ROM drive was easier than you thought it would be!

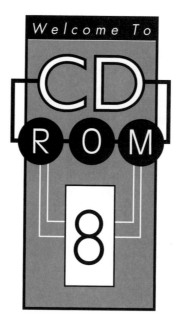

Welcome To

CD
ROM

8

BUILDING A
CD-ROM LIBRARY

In this lesson…

…A good cross-section of what's currently available on CD-ROM and
concise reviews of eighty-one excellent titles

…A few more terms used in conjunction with CD-ROM

With the snowballing popularity of CD-ROM and dropping prices for drives, it is fast becoming a consumer's market with regard to the quantity and diversity of CD-ROM titles available. Here are reviews of some products that will be of interest to CD-ROM users from preschool well into the senior years. With over 2,000 CD-ROM titles currently "in print," there's sure to be numerous discs of interest for everyone, no matter how diverse or eclectic the taste. I've included my reviews of eighty-one CD-ROM titles to give you an idea of the exciting "ocean of optical information" that awaits you.

Let me preface these reviews by saying that you won't find a bad review included here. That is by design, not by accident. To put it quite honestly, the space for this chapter was limited so I didn't want to waste it by covering anything that didn't represent an excellent CD-ROM value. Therefore, every one of the titles you see reviewed here is definitely worthwhile. Here's a listing of the titles reviewed in this lesson:

...About Cows

...A Christmas Carol

...African American Experience, The

...Aircraft Encyclopedia, The

...Amazing Moby, The

...American Civil War, The

...American Heritage Illustrated Encyclopedic Dictionary

...Aquatic Art

...Arthur's Teacher Trouble

...Best of MIDI Connection, The

...Best of Photography Volume 1, The

...Best of Sound Bytes Volume 1, The

...Between Heaven and Hell II

...Beyond The Wall of Stars

...Case of the Cautious Condor, The

...CD-ROM Directory—1992, The

...CD-ROMs in Print:1992

...CIA World Tour

...Classic Art Image Library Volume 1

...Compton's Family Choice

...Compton's Family Encyclopedia

...Compton's Multimedia Encyclopedia

...Corel Draw! 3.0

...Countries of the World

...Creation Stories

...Desktop Publishing 2.0

...Digital Gallery Limited

...Donatelli Portfolios: Lingerie, The

...Don Quixote

...Electronic Library of Art, The

...Exotica-ROM

...Family Doctor, The

...Funny: The Movie in QuickTime

...Goferwinkel's Adventures: The Lavender Land

...Great Literature

...Guinness Multimedia Disc of Records—1992

...Info-Power

...Jazz: A Multimedia History

...KGB-CIA World Factbook

...Klotski

...Library of the Future Series–Second Edition

...LIFEmap Series

...Line and The Shape Eater, The

...Lovely Ladies II

...Macmillan Dictionary for Children, The

...Magiclips Music

...Mammals: A Multimedia Encyclopedia

...Microsoft Bookshelf/1992

...Microsoft Cinemania

...Microsoft Musical Instruments

...Mother Earth II

...MPC Wizard

...Murder Makes Strange Deadfellows

...Murmurs of Earth

...Nautilus Monthly Magazine

...New Basics Electronic Cookbook, The

...New Grolier Multimedia Encyclopedia

...Phethean's Public Domain #2

...Prescription Drugs

...Presidents: It All Started with George, The

...Private Pictures I

...Seventh Wonder CD-ROM

...Software Jukebox

...Sports Illustrated CD-ROM Sports Almanac

...Sports ROM, The

...Talking Jungle Safari

...Talking Schoolhouse CD

...Time Table of History Series

...Total Baseball

...Twelve Roads to Gettysburg

...Ultima Underworld/Wing Commander II

...U.S.A. Factbook

...U.S.A. Wars: Desert Storm

…U.S. History on CD-ROM

…U.S. Presidents

…Where in the World is Carmen Sandiego/Deluxe

…Wild Places

…Wing Commander II Deluxe Edition

…Word Tales

…World Almanac and Book of Facts/1992

…WorldView

Before we get into the actual reviews of these CD-ROMs, there are a few additional terms that will be helpful to you in selecting titles for your personal library. In the format section of the review you'll see listings for PC, Mac, and MPC. The PC designation means the disc will work properly under MS-DOS—there's no need for the Windows operating environment or MPC-capable hardware. The Mac designation means the title is either Macintosh compatible or there is a separate Macintosh version of the disc available for Mac users. The MPC format designation means that the disc was designed to run on an MPC-compatible system and won't work properly (or at all) if it is used with a system that isn't MPC compliant.

Some discs have the code for both PC and Macintosh versions of the data on the same disc. These discs are known as *hybrid discs* since they contain the same data written in two different formats.

HYBRID DISC—a CD-ROM that has the data encoded in two formats so that it can be read by PC and Macintosh systems. The actual data is physically written in these discrete formats on separate locations on the CD-ROM.

Some CD-ROMs that have extensive text-based information may also have hypertext links to make accessing the information, or related topics, easy and automatic. Hypertext-linked information is usually presented in a contrasting color or underlined in the text so that it can be accessed simply by clicking the mouse upon the target word, term or phrase. At that point, the hypertext link will automatically jump to the linked information, whether it is text, picture, sound or video-based.

HYPERTEXT—a means of linking and presenting information using target words within the text as the "hot links" that trigger hypertext jumps. Using hypertext, related information (which may be textual, pictorial, audio or video in nature) can be accessed in a totally non-sequential way, permitting the user to jump about and explore topics of interest entirely at will.

There are several other terms that you'll find used throughout the following reviews, so here are the definitions for these terms now:

FRONT END—a term that is sometimes used to describe the user interface of a software product, it can also refer to the primary stage of a multi-stage hardware device.

TSR—an abbreviation for Terminate and Stay Resident, which denotes a type of program running under MS-DOS that remains loaded in memory even when it is not running so that it can be quickly invoked for a specific task while in another application.

EPS—an abbreviation for Encapsulated PostScript. A set of PostScript commands that can be used as an independent entity for data such as clip-art.

PUBLIC DOMAIN SOFTWARE—any program donated for public use by its owner or developer and freely available for copying and distribution.

 **SHAREWARE**—copyrighted software that is distributed free of charge but is usually accompanied by a request for a small payment from satisfied users to cover costs and registration for documentation and program updates.

 **CLIP-ART**—any collection of proprietary or public domain photographs, diagrams, maps, drawings, or other such graphics that can be "clipped" from the collection and incorporated into other documents or applications.

 TIF/TIFF—abbreviations for Tagged Image File Format, a standard bitmap file format commonly used for scanning, storage, and interchange of grayscale images.

 **BMP**—an abbreviation for bitmap, a data structure file format that describes a bit image by providing fixed coordinates for the X and Y axes of each pixel comprising the image. Bitmaps are commonly used as the filetypes for images created with many drawing, paint, and graphics software programs.

 **PIC/PICT**—a common bitmap filetype frequently used for storing image files such as scanned photos, graphics, and clip-art images.

 **PCX**—a very popular bitmap filetype developed by Z-Soft that is used for storing scanned photos, graphics, and images created with numerous draw, paint, and scanning applications software packages.

QUICKTIME—Apple Computer's proprietary means of playing compressed full-motion video images with synchronized sound. QuickTime is an extension to the Apple System Software.

HYPERCARD—software designed for the Apple Macintosh that provides users with an information management tool that uses a series of "cards" collected in a "stack." Each card represents a record for an individual item or data category and can contain text, graphical images and sound.

CD-ROM ACCESSORIES

You'll find that as your CD-ROM library grows you'll need some way to store the discs and make accessing them a bit easier and less cumbersome. While an old shoe box or other such container would suffice in a pinch, investing a few dollars in a dedicated accessory certainly provides additional ergonomic and organizational advantages over "roughing it."

If you have a CD-ROM drive that uses caddies, then you'll want to purchase some additional caddies to make swapping discs faster and to reduce the amount of physical handling of the discs themselves. Universal CD-ROM caddies are available from QB products for $12.99 each as well as from other manufacturers (quantity discounts may be available).

Storage of your optical software can be accomplished in a variety of ways. There are many audio CD storage racks available that can serve double-duty for CD-ROM storage as well. Here are some examples to give you an idea of what's available:

...QB products offers a basic plastic disc storage box that can sit on a desk or be wall mounted for $6.99 each as well as a cubic spring-loaded disc storage unit that pops-out the desired disc for $14.99. For more advanced libraries, the company also has the TurnFile/CD, a lazy-susan type of rotary file module with swivel base that can hold up to sixty discs for $64.00. Additional add-on modules, priced at $55.00

each, can be attached to the basic unit to increase capacity as your needs increase.

...The Discwasher CD Storage System is a flip-rack system that can hold up to twenty discs. The rack can sit on top of a desk or be wall-mounted if desired. The suggested list price for the CD Storage System is $20.00 per unit.

...You might also want to consider a CD cleaning unit, especially if your drive doesn't use caddies and you have lots of fingerprints on your CD-ROMs. Many good units are available, such as the battery-operated Discwasher non-contact CD HydroBath, which carries a suggested list price of $59.95.

FIGURE 8.1 *Accessories can make using CD-ROM easier and more productive. Extra caddies (shown in the foreground above) reduce disc handling and make swapping CD-ROMs faster. CD-ROMs in jewel cases or caddies can be stored in several ways, and three are shown above: (left) the disc-cube from QB designs holds ten CD-ROMs and features a spring-loaded serving mechanism to eject the desired disc(s); (center) QB's lazy-susan TurnFile/CD holds up to fifteen discs in each of four compartments, rotates to provide access; (right) Discwasher CD Storage System is a flip-rack that holds twenty CDs or CD-ROMs and can be wall-mounted or used on a desktop as shown above.*

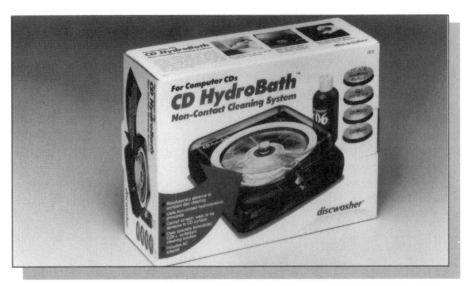

FIGURE 8.2 *The Discwasher Computer CD HydroBath non-contact cleaning system is shown above. Intended for use with all types of computer compact discs including CD-ROM, CD-I, Photo CD, and audio CDs, the system uses a special fluid that is pumped under pressure onto the playing surface while it is rotating at high speed to clean the disc without any rubbing or abrasion.*

I've made every attempt to ensure that the information listed here for pricing and format availability is accurate, however many of the publishers intend to release their titles in additional formats in the near future. Bear that in mind as you read these reviews; even if the format you desire isn't listed as being available as of this writing, it may well be available in your desired format by the time you read this.

The same applies to the manufacturer's suggested list prices that are printed here. Prices usually drop to make products more accessible as consumer demand increases, and CD-ROMs are no exception. I strongly recommend that you check with the publishers (you'll find their names, addresses, and phone numbers listed in Appendix D) to check on format availability and current pricing.

CD-ROM REVIEW

Title: *About Cows*
Format(s): *PC and Mac*
Publisher: *Quanta Press*
List Price: *$29.95*

If you've ever wondered about or marveled at the gentle cud-chewing mobile mammal dairy bars we call cows, then this disc is a must-have for your library. One of the first CD-ROMs to be mass produced and marketed, it is also one of the flagship products that put Quanta Press "on the map" as a major publishing force in the world of CD-ROM.

FIGURE 8.3 *This bovine beauty is wearing shades and traveling incognito thanks to the fame her picture in About Cows has produced. Thirty-two high-resolution pictures of cows are included in both color and black-and-white versions on the CD-ROM.*

Based on the book by Sara Lindsay Rath, this CD-ROM features scores of anecdotes, bovine history, cow trivia, folk lore, and an amazing array of facts about this wonderful beast that has been called "the original vending machine." Thirty-two photos (color and black-and-white versions are both included) of cows in various poses and locales augment this classic text on these animals. Wonderfully entertaining and educational, it's a delight for CD-ROM users of any age.

CD-ROM
REVIEW

Title: A Christmas Carol
Format(s): MPC
Publisher: Ebook, Inc.
List Price: $49.95

"There's more of gravy than of grave about you, whatever you are!" declared Ebenezer Scrooge, the insufferable curmudgeon who is the central character of Charles Dickens' immortal classic. The tale springs to life in this CD-ROM version of the famous holiday literary work.

In addition to the full text of *A Christmas Carol*, Ebook has provided twenty-seven color and black-and-white illustrations by Sir Arthur Rackham to illuminate the story and provide some visual diversion.

From an audio perspective, this multimedia storybook is rich and entertaining with a fully narrated automatic reading of the story. This makes *A Christmas Carol* easy to enjoy even while using the computer for other tasks while the story is read unobtrusively in the background.

Eight favorite Christmas carols are also included in full stereo on the CD-ROM as well, and they can also be played on any standard audio CD player.

To make understanding the story easier, a hypertext-linked on-screen dictionary provides concise definitions as well as an index and learning guide to make using and getting the most from the CD-ROM easy. It is important to note that this is an MPC CD-ROM title which requires proper hardware (MPC-compliant to access all of the software's features and for satisfactory playback). Recommended for all ages, it makes an excellent seasonal title to give or receive.

CD-ROM REVIEW

Title: African American Experience, The
Format(s): PC
Publisher: Quanta Press
List Price: $129.00

This CD-ROM is touted as an "electronic textbook" that tells the compelling history of African Americans beginning with their origins in the African homeland. Using the IBM Linkway graphical user interface, the work incorporates multimedia features including sound, narrative and high-resolution color pictures.

Africa has been called the birthplace of civilization, and this CD-ROM takes the user on a cultural journey predating Christ by several millennia, through the age of iron, and into the migration to America.

All elements of African American history are explored in great detail, relying in major part on "telling the story" in the words, perspectives and, in many cases, in the actual voices of African Americans themselves.

Topics on the CD-ROM include: the African continent, explorers, freedom fighters, politics, biographies, profiles of black scientists/artists/notable African Americans, culture, and social life. Scores of color and black-and-white photos augment the text and audio tracks and bring the story to life.

The audio portions of the disc can be heard by plugging a pair of headphones or extension speakers into the CD-ROM drives headphone jack, so no internal audio card is required in the PC for audio playback.

An important and impressive work from cultural and educational standpoints, this CD-ROM is an exemplary reference work on African American history through the ages.

CD-ROM REVIEW

Title: *Aircraft Encyclopedia, The*
Format(s): *PC*
Publisher: *Quanta Press*
List Price: *$69.95*

If you're an aircraft buff, or someone who just wants to have a superb collection of aircraft photographs along with all of the attendant specifications, then this CD-ROM title is a must-have addition for your optical library.

Described as a visual compendium of worldwide aircraft, this disc contains hundreds of black-and-white pictures as well as full-color super VGA images of all types of aircraft. Just about every conceivable flying genre is included in this collection, from passenger aircraft to the high-tech Stealth craft used by U.S. forces with such decisive success in the Persian Gulf War.

Line drawings and full descriptions of each aircraft's unique capabilities and developmental history are also included.

FIGURE 8.4 *The Stealth Bomber is just one of the unique and remarkable aircraft which is profiled in great detail on Quanta Press's The Aircraft Encyclopedia. The CD-ROM contains color VGA and Super VGA images as well as B/W TIFF files of aircraft of all descriptions.*

CD-ROM REVIEW

Title: Amazing Moby, The
Format(s): PC
Publisher: Alde Publishing
List Price: $395.00

Words—lots of them—are what *The Amazing Moby* is all about. Intended primarily as a base lexicon for constructing spell-checkers, hyphenators, and other word-processing utilities for programmers and software application developers, this CD-ROM is also a superb treasure trove of information on syllabilization, hyphenation, parts of speech, and pronunciation.

The CD-ROM is divided into four subdirectories, one each for hyphenation, parts of speech, pronunciation, and words. The main the content of these subdirectories is reflected in their respective names and is divided as follows: *Moby Words* is a word/phrase list of more than 500,000 entries. *Moby Hyphenator* gives you over 150,000 words fully hyphenated/syllabified. *Moby Pronunciator* has 150,000 words and phrases encoded with full pronunciation, using standard pronunciation phonemes as published by the IPA. *Moby Parts of Speech* provides over 200,000 words and phrases, each described by prioritized part(s) of speech.

Since all of the information contained on the CD-ROM is alphabetically arranged in list format, there isn't too much required to use the disc. Everything you need to know is contained on "readme" files on the CD-ROM itself.

The Amazing Moby is the biggest straight ASCII source of lexical information in the world, and it makes an excellent data source for software programmers, educators, linguists or virtually any CD-ROM user who is interested in words, their spelling and pronunciation.

CD-ROM REVIEW

Title: *American Civil War, The*
Format(s): *PC and Mac*
Publisher: *Quanta Press*
List Price: *$69.95*

Virtually any type of information you could desire on the Civil War is contained on this disc including biographies of key figures, statistics, chronology, equipment, campaigns, battles, foreign involvement, and more is covered in depth and detail.

A full bibliography is also included as well as information on the political climate and important people of the era, along with a huge collection of color and black-and-white photos.

As an added bonus, the last twelve tracks are audio selections of homespun music of the Civil War era. Played on period musical instruments (including banjo, guitar, dulcimer, fife, and drum) by Bobby Horton, these tunes are also playable on a standard audio CD-player as well.

FIGURE 8.5 *Union soldiers pose proudly with their cannon in one of the scores of authentic period photos included on the American Civil War CD-ROM from Quanta Press. Twelve audio tracks of music from the Civil War era are also included as an added bonus.*

CD-ROM REVIEW

Title: **American Heritage Illustrated Encylopedic Dictionary**
Format(s): **PC**
Publisher: **Xiphias**
List Price: **$79.95**

Words are the essence of human communication and, as such, should not be taken lightly. This disc gives words—lots of them—the attention they so rightly deserve, and in the process provides a dynamic reference work that is of value to the student, business, or home computer user.

Based on the highly-regarded *American Heritage Illustrated Dictionary* published by Houghton Mifflin, this multimedia reference includes over 180,000 definitions and thousands of colorful pictures.

You can look-up a word without knowing the exact spelling simply by selecting the first few letters of that word on the lookup screen and hitting the search button. A list of words that begin with those letters displays in seconds.

You can browse by paging from definition to definition or use the powerful "hot word" (hypertext) searching facility to call-up all definitions associated with a word selected in the text.

Your family's vocabulary will rapidly increase as you chart new pathways through the richness of the English language. This disc makes discovering a wealth of words fun as well as educational. The kids will be especially fond of it, since it takes the drudgery out of spelling and definition homework assignments.

Versions are also available for Commodore CDTV and Tandy/ Memorex VIS, also at a suggested list price of $79.95 per format.

CD-ROM REVIEW

Title: Aquatic Art
Format(s): PC and Mac
Publisher: Gazelle Technologies
List Price: $149.95

A marvelous collection of over 200 sparkling images of marine life from Hawaii and the Caribbean constitutes the content of this CD-ROM.

Since this is a hybrid disk, it's readable by Macintosh and IBM-compatible PCs so you can use it with either machine type with any software that can support TIFF files.

Macintosh users can take advantage of the included HyperCard interface that permits previewing the photos in color. A Mac II, LC or SE/30 with color monitor, CD-ROM drive, 24-bit color video card, and 5MB of RAM are the suggested requirements for using this disc at the highest level on a Mac. A Photoshop software demo is also included on the disc, as well as a copy of HyperCard 2.0 for Mac users.

While the subject matter may be "all wet" the quality of the photos is certainly not. Sea horses, crabs, coral, sea urchins, octopi, sharks, tropical fish, marvelous underwater plant life, and more are all covered on this disc in dazzling full-color photography.

Unlimited reproduction rights are granted with the disc, so you can use any of the images any way you desire without incurring a usage fee or royalty payment. This disc will prove to be an invaluable resource for any type of graphic arts or presentation work that would benefit from excellent underwater photography. Whether you're a designer or just love to look at excellent photos of underwater life, this is a prize catch!

CD-ROM REVIEW

Title: **Arthur's Teacher Trouble**
Format(s): **Mac**
Publisher: **Broderbund**
List Price: **$59.95**

One of Broderbund's *Living Books* titles, this is a wonderful disc for young CD-ROM users between the ages of 6 to 10.

The program content is marvelously interactive and provides fertile ground for young minds to exercise both their imagination and curiosity. Clicking on items contained in the on-screen pictures trigger actions that keep interest levels high while providing entertainment.

As both an educational and recreational product, *Arthur's Teacher Trouble* excels in these two areas. The narrative and instructions are included in both English or Spanish for bilingual access. Youngsters can choose to have the story automatically read to them, or play and explore each "page" of the book and the items it contains. The various items on the pages are also triggers for events. Clicking on an item (a bell, for example) will cause it to ring. Clicking on the ball icon at the beginning of a sentence causes the entire sentence to be read out loud as the text being read is highlighted so the youngster can follow along.

The story is by Marc Brown, an award-winning author of books for children. Brown has written and illustrated over 100 books and is best-known for his popular *Arthur Adventures* (a print copy of this colorful book that is the basis for the CD-ROM is also included as an added bonus). By the time you read this an MPC version of this and other Broderbund *Living Books* will be available for non-Macintosh users as well.

CD-ROM REVIEW

Title: **Best of MIDI Connection, The**
Format(s): **MPC and Mac**
Publisher: **Metatec Corp./Discovery Systems**
List Price: **$49.95**

Like its sister products *The Best of Photography* and *The Best of Sound Bytes, The Best of MIDI Connection* is a compilation of material that has been used in the *Nautilus* monthly CD-ROM "magazine" from Metatec/Discovery Systems, but there's lots of additional material here that is new and unique to this disc.

The CD-ROM is a hybrid disc so it plays correctly in either a Macintosh or an IBM-compatible computer (the files appear in two formats on discrete locations on the disc). Over 300 MIDI files are provided for use by both Macintosh and DOS/Windows sequencer software.

The selection provides a pleasantly rich variety of classical, ragtime, and contemporary compositions that vary in scope from single instrument pieces to full orchestral, multi-timbral works of considerable complexity.

Ready-to-use drum patterns and chord progressions are included as "building blocks" for the MIDI composer, and improvisation aids with EPS (Encapsulated PostScript) printable sheet music are also useful features of this disc.

All of the MIDI files on the disc were saved in two formats: Passport Designs *MasterTracks/Pro4* format and as standard MIDI files ready for import into your favorite MIDI software for playback, arranging or editing.

There's also a digital audio preview capability provided for both Macintosh and MPC users (MPC-compatible hardware is required on IBM-compatibles). This disc is an excellent MIDI resource.

Title: *Best of Photography Volume 1, The*
Format(s): *MPC and Mac*
Publisher: *Metatec Corp./Discovery Systems*
List Price: *$49.95*

Like the other titles in Metatec/Discovery's *Best Of* series, this disc, too, is a collection of material that was originally included in past issues of *Nautilus,* the monthly multimedia CD-ROM information service, as well as image files that will appear in future issues.

This CD-ROM is a hybrid disc, meaning that it contains the proper file formats for Macintosh computers as well as for Windows-equipped IBM-compatible PCs.

Over fifty photos are included in this compendium and they can be used without paying any royalty for non-commercial uses.

Subject matter ranges from relaxing water-front and countryside scenes to barns and towers, churches, stadiums, and more. The images make excellent background visuals for multimedia presentations, desktop publishing, and as cel backgrounds for higher-end animation programs.

Images are provided in color 8-bit PICT and 24-bit TIFF formats for the Macintosh user, while color 8-bit PIC, GIF, DIB and 24-bit TIF file formats are provided for the PC user. Microsoft Windows is required for the PC version.

Much of the imagery contained on this CD-ROM was selected because of its unique expression, cultural or historical influence, as well as for its visual beauty. If your intended applications and uses may require excellent stock photography, this *Best Of* collection is a title that may provide just the shot you're looking for.

CD-ROM REVIEW

Title: Best of Sound Bytes Volume 1, The
Format(s): MPC and Mac
Publisher: Metatec Corp./Discovery Systems
List Price: $49.95

Available in separate versions for both MPC and Macintosh computers, this disc is a diverse collection of music, sounds, audio tracks, and waveform sound files compiled from over a dozen issues of *Nautilus,* a Macintosh and Windows/MPC CD-ROM monthly "optical media magazine" service (see the *Nautilus* review).

Both versions contain twenty multimedia music beds, twelve sound effects, two 60-second spots. 60-, 30-, 15- and 5-second multimedia music beds are also provided.

The Macintosh version contains files that are compatible with the DigiDesign AudioMedia System card or the Macromind/Paracomp Soundedit System, and an interactive listing and "locator" front-end for the sound files is provided. All of the sound files have been recorded in four formats and are provided in 44kHz, 22kHz, and 11kHz sampling rates.

The MPC version has files that are compatible with all Windows-supported MPC-compatible audio devices. All of the sound files on this version are recorded in two formats: 22kHz 8-bit (.WAV file format) and 44kHz 16-bit (.AIF file format). A "locator" listing of all sound files on the disc is included.

Sounds include high quality recordings of such effects as bowling balls hitting pins and jet planes flying-by overhead. Excellent musical beds in various pre-timed durations make assembling the background audio portion of a multimedia presentation or movie a snap. And all of the audio can be used royalty-free!

Title: *Between Heaven and Hell II*
Format(s): *PC*
Publisher: *Bureau Development, Inc.*
List Price: *$99.00*

This disc contains the entire text of the *King James Edition of the Bible* and promptly moves into more worldly and material pursuits, hence its name. With a total of 12,109 files on the disc you'll be hard-pressed to find a better CD-ROM value, with content that includes dozens of great games such as *Risk, Spacewar, Puzzle, Crypto, Monopoly* and *Trivia*; a broad selection of graphic images, including those of normal and not-so-normal people in varying seductive poses (don't worry folks—nothing really offensive here) as well as images of the less-earthy type; two different image display programs for viewing the images; lots of arcane but useful programs like chemistry tutors, calorie counters, a federal building life-cycle cost calculator, and more.

But wait—there's more! In addition to all of this you get hundreds of shareware programs including such unusual goodies as extended disk managers, a family history tracking system as well as communications software, tickler/appointment trackers and lot's of other interesting stuff including a runtime version of a hypertext development system!

To help navigate through the disc the Norton NCD command can be quickly called-up since the TREEINFO file has already been stored on the disc. This means you'll be able to see the entire directory structure of this CD-ROM in seconds and it gives you a complete graphic picture of the subdirectory tree. A copy of the *Still River Shell* is also included to facilitate file transfers from the CD-ROM to floppies or a hard drive.

CD-ROM REVIEW

Title: **Beyond The Wall of Stars**
Format(s): **MPC**
Publisher: **Creative Multimedia Corporation**
List Price: **$49.99**

Beyond The Wall of Stars is the first in CMC's *Taran Trilogy* of CD-ROM-based multimedia interactive adventures. R.A. Montgomery, author of the adventure, is also the author and creator of the *Choose-Your-Own-Adventure* series of books published by Bantam. This series has become very popular with children and young adults because it allows them to explore the consequences of different plot twists and endings (hence the "choose your own adventure" series title). Since their initial publication in 1980, worldwide sales of Montgomery's books now exceed 40 million copies and the series has been translated into thirty-eight languages.

This disc is the first CMC product to include three-dimensional animation, SVGA (640x480x256-color) graphics, sound, games, simulations, and text to totally immerse the user in the adventure. This adventure introduces a new vocabulary and extensive references to concepts of science and mythology. It also includes an "electronic bookmark" that allows the user to save the adventure at any point along the way, so you can experiment with various options and still return to a particular decision point. This feature is excellent for those gamesters who like to carefully and thoroughly ponder all of their options before committing to a particular course of action.

This disc complies with the MPC specification and MPC hardware is required for proper playback of the software. If you like adventure games this will be an excellent choice for you.

Title: *Case of the Cautious Condor, The*
Format(s): *PC and MPC*
Publisher: *Tiger Media*
List Price: *$49.95*

If you are an adventure game aficionado and you have the right hardware, you'll be very interested in Tiger Media's first Airwave Adventure, *The Case of the Cautious Condor.*

Like its companion title in the Airwave Adventure series, *Murder Makes Strange Deadfellows* (see that review as well), *The Case of the Cautious Condor* requires a SoundBlaster, SoundBlaster Pro, or ThunderBoard audio card in the PC for the DOS version to work correctly. Also note that the MPC version of the game requires MPC-compliant hardware to run under Windows.

The game is a 1930's-style murder mystery interactive drama that takes you on a journey with private eye Ned Peters. Along the way you'll meet a colorful cast of international suspects and you'll have thirty minutes to examine the evidence, establish means, opportunity, motive, and solve the murder.

Since the disc contains hundreds of images and hours of audio, there are thousands of possible ways for the adventure to go...but only one solution.

In addition to dazzling graphics, excellent production values and great plot twists, the CD-ROM also contains over twenty-one minutes of Red Book Audio so you can enjoy the musical selections on any audio CD player when you're not playing the game (track 1 is computer data and should not be played through speakers).

If you're still not sold on *The Case of the Cautious Condor*, consider this: it was named "best hit software" by Japan's leading PC Magazine.

Title: **CD-ROM Directory—1992, The**
Format(s): **PC**
Publisher: **UniDisc, Inc.**
List Price: **$220/year**

This disc is the optical-media counterpart of the printed directory that has been published annually by TFPL Ltd. in the United Kingdom. UniDisc, based in California, publishes the CD-ROM version. It is published twice (January and June) yearly.

The disc provides comprehensive details on all CD-ROM and multimedia titles currently available. Information is provided on all companies involved in any aspect of the CD-ROM industry as well as information on hardware and software products, relevant conferences, exhibitions, books and journals.

International in its coverage, this disc is an invaluable reference work on the CD-ROM industry and a disc that I found to be indispensable in preparing this book.

```
The CD-ROM Directory 1992 (Companies) - KAwareF (tm) Fielded V1.30L-U
  F1 = Help     F2 = Options    F3 = Select     F4 = Search     F5 = Sets

                              Comprehensive Index
                              Company Name
                              Company Description
                              Field Of Activity
  Set   #Found   (Page 1 of 1) Contact Name and Title
                              CD-ROM Titles
                              Address
                              Country
                              Hardware Produced
                              Software Produced
                                   (1 of 14)




              (Ctrl-PgUp/PgDn changes Set List page)

       SEARCH SET=0   OUTPUT SET=0   WORKSPACE: 256000

  F6=Display   F7=Group ↓   F8=Group ↑   F9=Group ↓   F10=Exit   ESC=Backup
```

FIGURE 8.6 Information on the CD-ROM Directory can be searched by numerous criteria. This disc has everything you could need to know about the CD-ROM industry.

CD-ROM REVIEW

Title: CD-ROMS in Print: 1992
Format(s): PC/Mac
Publisher: Meckler
List Price: $95.00

If you're looking for a resource on CD-ROM to find out what's available on optical media this disc is a definite "must have" and it makes an excellent starting point for building your CD-ROM library. I personally find it to be an invaluable reference tool, and it was, in fact, a significant help in putting this chapter together.

The CD-ROM version is the optical counterpart of the printed book, but offers significant advantages thanks to the powerful search and retrieve capabilities of the personal computer.

Each of the over 3,500 title records and over 3,500 company records in the database is searchable. The main title entry record is searchable by up to twenty-seven information variables, and it uses Nimbus Information Systems' excellent *Romware* search software to make locating the data you seek easy.

Products are multiply-indexed to make searching by different criteria easy and fast. CD-ROM, CD-I, CDTV, and Electronic Book products are all covered in this database, and you can select or search based on the title, hardware requirements, application type, price, language, search software, and more. Company information can be searched or selected based on name, country, area, activities, and more.

Additionally a full global text search is also implemented on the disc so you can merely enter a key word, words or phrase and let the computer find every instances that matches. If you're serious about CD-ROM, this disc is indispensable.

CD-ROM REVIEW

Title: **CIA World Tour**
Format(s): **MPC**
Publisher: **Compton's New Media**
List Price: **$99.00**

In addition to this MPC version, this disc is also available for PC and Macintosh computers under the title *Multimedia World Fact Book*, also at a suggested retail price of $99.00.

Whether you're planning a coup in a South American dictatorship or just checking the terrain in Kuwait for a cloak-and-dagger meeting, the CIA has all of the information you'll need to plan your moves. This disc is, in fact, a product of the CIA itself: the *World Fact Book* is produced annually by the Central Intelligence Agency for the use of United States Government officials, so you can be sure of getting accurate information. By the way, information on this disc is *not* classified.

The MPC version includes actual performances of national anthem segments and color maps from Hammond, Incorporated that are acknowledged as the best available on microcomputers.

Detailed information is provided in 248 country profiles which include geography, maritime claims, disputes, climate, terrain, natural resources, land use, people, population (including birth and death rate, life expectancy, ethnic divisions, religion), language, literacy, labor force, government, GNP, inflation rate, unemployment, budget, exports, imports, debt, industrial production, industries, agriculture, aid, currency, communications, railroads, national holidays, military manpower, highways, inland waterways, pipelines, ports, civil air, defense forces, political pressure groups, diplomatic representation, suffrage, and much, much more.

CD-ROM REVIEW

Title: *Classic Art Image Library Volume I*
Format(s): *Mac*
Publisher: *G&G Designs/Communications*
List Price: *$199.00*

G&G Designs/Communications has been a leading producer of art and broadcast design graphics for television broadcasters. With years of experience in on-line satellite delivery of full-color computer illustrations to television stations and newspapers, G&G has created it's first product for the publishing and presentation industries with *Volume I* in the *Classic Art Image Library* series.

Classic Art is an image library consisting of numerous volumes of images. Each volume illustrates a specific topic. *Volume I*, the premiere collection, focuses on business. Future volumes will include health and medicine, environment, education, entertainment, and other themes for the artwork.

Like clip art, the artwork contained on *Classic Art* is licensed for unlimited reproduction including manipulation by the purchaser, with the exception that *Classic Art* may not be reproduced and sold as an art service.

All of the images are ready for use in desktop publishing, presentations, multimedia, and video production. Three file formats for each image are contained on the CD-ROM including 24-bit color TIFF, 24-bit color PICT, and 8-bit grayscale TIFF.

The images are truly "broadcast quality" graphics of the same caliber you regularly see on local and national evening news, weather and sportscasts. For high-end applications where something more than clip-art is required, *Classic Art* may have what you're looking for.

CD-ROM REVIEW

Title: *Compton's Family Choice*
Format(s): PC
Publisher: *Compton's New Media*
List Price: $149.95

Fifteen—that's right, fifteen—software applications representing a total retail value of over $600 if purchased separately on magnetic media is what *Compton's Family Choice CD-ROM* is all about. And, as the "family" part of the name infers, there's something for everyone in the household here.

Youngsters will love *The Berenstain Bears Learn About Counting* and *The Berenstain Bears Junior Jigsaw* as well as *Super Spellicopter* and *Math Maze*. The whole family will enjoy *States and Traits, Millionaire II, Revolution '76,* and *Designasaurus,* which represent fun and learning for all ages.

Just The Fax is a novel program for creating fax cover sheets and fax messages that are sure to be noticed, while *Grammar Examiner* puts you in the role of a newspaper editor and can support multiple players. In *Body Transparent,* a learning and trivia game, you'll explore nature's most incredible machine, the human body. *Algebra I First Semester* and *Algebra I Second Semester* is presented lucidly for the secondary student in these step-by-step learning programs that are more closely tied to today's school textbooks than any other algebra software.

The Fiction Advisor will generate a list of books and authors based on your particular interests so you'll never have to judge a book by its cover again.

A game the whole family can enjoy, *Jigsaw!* may be the ultimate electronic puzzle, and it allows you to make and save your own puzzles, too.

CD-ROM REVIEW

Title: Compton's Family Encyclopedia
Format(s): PC
Publisher: Compton's New Media
List Price: $695.00

Compton's claims that this disc has more articles from more volumes—enhanced with more pictures, more sound and more features—than any other publishers' CD-ROM encyclopedia. When you consider that it contains all twenty-six complete volumes of Compton's print encyclopedia, the complete 65,000-word *Webster's Intermediate Dictionary*, over 121,000 hypertext links, 31,000 articles, 10,000 pictures, an interactive *World Atlas*, music, speech, and sound, this claim certainly seems to be justified.

The encyclopedia provides all of the features and handy utilities you would expect from Compton's including electronic bookmarks, a savable notebook, cut and paste capability, a print option and an on-line help button. The extra features like the interactive atlas and the on-line dictionary—all hypertext-linked—that really make *CFE* a pleasure to use.

The user interface is extraordinarily friendly, permitting you to ask questions in your own words (such as, "Why is the sky blue?") and presenting the correct answer with related information. You can also browse through the pictures or listen to music, speech and more by simply pointing and clicking with the mouse.

You can spin the on-screen globe and stop it anywhere you desire. If you zoom-in on a continent, country, city or mountain peak you'll automatically be presented with and linked to all available information on the disc about it—all with the simple click of a button!

Title: *Compton's MultiMedia Encyclopedia*
Format(s): *PC and Mac*
Publisher: *Compton's New Media*
List Price: *$695.00/$795.00*

This new version of this innovative, award-winning CD-ROM title is now optimized to take advantage of the Microsoft Windows environment and multimedia capabilities. The disc contains all twenty-six volumes of the *Compton's Encyclopedia* in print: 9 million words in 32,000 articles, 1,000 images, maps and graphs, and 5,000 charts and diagrams, plus 60 minutes of music, speech, and other sounds as well as forty-three animated sequences. Without a doubt, this is one of the most information-laden CD-ROMs currently available.

Additionally, the complete *Webster's Intermediate Dictionary* is also contained on the CD-ROM and is available on-line while using the software. Multiple text and picture windows are supported, and selected articles are augmented with animation sequences to increase understanding and retention of the material.

The disc utilizes Compton's highly effective yet easy-to-use search and retrieval engine. Full Boolean searches are supported, and a "bookmark" feature allows you to backtrack through complex searches to arrive at the initial starting point.

The audio portions of the disc play through the CD-ROM drive's headphone jack or audio outputs if your PC doesn't have a sound card. Windows is required, however, and the PC should have a minimum of 2MB of RAM available. A Macintosh version of this disc is also available for $795.00 suggested list, and a Macintosh LC or better with 4MB of RAM and a 12 inch or larger color monitor is required to run this version, along with System 6.0.7 or later.

Title: CorelDraw! 3.0
Format(s): PC (Windows)
Publisher: Corel Corporation
List Price: $749.95

CorelDraw! 3.0 is an entire art and graphics design studio all on a single CD-ROM, and that's not an exaggeration, either!

The system requirements for this professional-level package are on the heavy side and a minimum of 4MB of RAM is required to run this Windows 3.1-compatible application. A mouse or graphics tablet and a Windows-supported VGA monitor round out the hardware requirements. Under Windows 3.1 the True Type font support is enabled, while font support relies on Adobe Type Manager (not included) if *CorelDraw* is run under Windows 3.0.

In addition to *CorelDraw*, the world's leading vector-based drawing and illustration program, the CD-ROM disc also contains *CorelTrace* (a bitmap tracing utility), *CorelMosaic* (a visual file manager for graphics files), *CorelChart* (a charting and pictograph application), *CorelShow* (an easy to use program for creating polished presentations) and *CorelPhoto-Paint* (a sophisticated retouching and editing application capable of supporting 24-bit true color).

If that's not enough for you, then consider that the CD-ROM also contains over 250 True Type and Type 1 fonts, 12,000 clipart and symbol images, scores of chart templates, *CorelPhoto-Paint* samples, and sample "flicks" (presentations and animations).

The documentation is excellent in helping you get the most from these programs, which all feature on-line help. A bonus videotape is also provided to give you a quick introduction.

Title: Countries of the World
Format(s): PC and Mac
Publisher: Bureau Development, Inc.
List Price: $495.00

Billed by Bureau as "the ultimate international reference—the equivalent of 250,000 pages," this descriptor is probably accurate. *Countries of the World* includes the full text of all 106 U.S. Army Country Series Handbooks, maps, color flags of every country, national anthems (actual audio recordings), and hundreds of pages of detailed bibliographic information. Topics covered for each country include the historical setting, society, environment, economy, government, politics, and national security.

Countries of the World also includes high-resolution color maps by Hammond, Incorporated (the leader in cartography). These maps cover the entire boundaries, population, climate, ocean contours, vegetation, agriculture, mining, energy, and land use. Information is provided by the U.S. embassies of 151 countries to ensure that it is current and accurate. The sheer volume and range of material on this disc is unmatched, according to the publisher, by any atlas, encyclopedia or reference in any format.

A simple user interface makes it easy to browse through this vast collection of country study books, print specific articles or chapters and instantly search by word, event, book, picture, or article. This disc is a fantastic resource for market researchers, libraries, schools, international travelers, business people, government officials, or anyone else whose interests extend beyond the borders of the United States. It is an absolutely invaluable reference disc of international proportions.

CD-ROM REVIEW

Title: Creation Stories
Format(s): MPC
Publisher: Warner New Media
List Price: $49.95

Human beings have inhabited this planet for about 250,000 years. In that time there have been thousands of cultural groups—diverse societal bands that composed extended families, tribes, even nations. Each group has wondered about the beginning of life. Without exception, every group, from the Aboriginal to the scientific, has attempted to explain its origins.

This disc is divided into six sections covering an entire cycle of creation legend, including the beginning and arrangement of the world, the creation of humans, the intrusion of disharmony and the destruction and rebirth of the world.

There are twelve stories to listen to and eighty-one more to read. Often a creation story may tell more about the people who told the story than about creation itself.

Throughout these tales you'll find startling similarities and intriguing differences among our perceptions of the world and its beginnings. The great unity, however, is the wonder and awe all cultures have felt at the miracle of creation.

This disc is as beautiful to look at as it is to listen to. The high-resolution photos and imagery complement the excellent narratives and audio effects to impart a very dramatic sense to the subject matter.

A substantial amount of free hard disk space (2MB or more) is desirable for copying the images for the desired story so that the audio can proceed without interruptions. This is an MPC disc and full MPC-compliant hardware is required for proper operation.

CD-ROM REVIEW

Title: Desktop Publishing 2.0
Format(s): Mac
Publisher: Gazelle Technologies
List Price: $99.95

If you're a designer, graphic artist, or page layout artist you'll find this disc to be an invaluable resource in your work that can elevate your plain pages into digital masterpieces!

This CD-ROM contains over 1,600 EPS clip-art files, over 300 laser fonts in Type 3, Type 1, and True Type format, Educorp's Graphic Designs clip-art volumes 1 to 5, aircraft EPS graphics, stamps of the world in color and grayscale and utilities specifically designed for desktop publishing use.

A Macintosh Plus or higher model equipped with a CD-ROM drive, a hard drive and a minimum of 2MB of RAM is required to use this disc.

In addition to the fonts and artwork that can be used royalty-free, the disc also contains a HyperCard browser to facilitate previewing the fonts and clip-art as well as for copying files and folders to the hard drive. If you desire, you can also assemble a "slide show" with the included utilities for the clip-art or fonts to create running displays.

Demos of *Photoshop, TypeStyler,* and other programs related to graphics and desktop publishing are also included on the disc as well as the *Educorp Sampler,* a collection of other titles available from Educorp.

The images are excellent quality and cover a wide range of subjects and the font collection alone more than justifies the purchase price of this disc for any Macintosh-based desktop publishing or graphics applications.

CD-ROM REVIEW

Title: Digital Gallery Limited/Monthly
Format(s): Mac
Publisher: Digital Gallery Limited
List Price: $150/edition

This CD-ROM is for anyone who needs very high-end stock photo images that are ready for pre-press and output to an imagesetter or page output device. This is not typical stock photography or clip art, but sophisticated images of selected subjects provided in very high-resolution formats.

The *Digital Gallery Limited Monthly Editions* are only produced in quantities of 1,000 per edition, so the user-base for these pictures will be limited to this figure. Unlike other stock photography resources that do not limit their production quantities, the DGL images have an immediate edge in their limited access. As with vintage wine, only the discriminating few will forego the expense to obtain the best.

Each month a new disc with all new images is produced, so the subject matter will vary with each new edition. The premiere edition, for example, contained the following twenty high-resolution photos: forest panoramic, vintage rural, desert panoramic, mountain lake, fog lake panoramic, river sunset, waterfront park, perspective corridor, pastoral barn, summer carnival, cityscape sunset, forest stream, beached ship, night bridge, city buildings, winter river, loading dock, urban skyline, spring parkway, and ocean surf. As you can see by this example, the subject matter is quite diverse.

Each photo is scanned and color-corrected for 7x10 inches at a 175-line screen and there is no use royalty.

CD-ROM REVIEW

Title: **Donatelli Portfolios: Lingerie, The**
Format(s): **PC and Mac**
Publisher: **Gazelle Technologies**
List Price: **$99.95**

Here's a collection of 100 high-quality photos of twenty professional models in various types of lingerie that can be used without paying for expensive stock photography or modeling fees.

With this disc it's as simple as clicking a mouse to add a touch of beauty and glamour to ads, brochures and calendars using the photos contained in this portfolio. You can use the photos just as they are or you can create your own graphics and illustrations using them as the base reference images.

This is a hybrid disc that works on a Macintosh or IBM-compatible PC equipped with a CD-ROM drive.

FIGURE 8.7 Dawn, shown above, is one of the twenty beautiful professional models appearing in the Donatelli Portfolio on Lingerie from Gazelle Technologies. These shots can be used royalty-free.

CD-ROM REVIEW

Title: *Don Quixote*
Format(s): *MPC*
Publisher: *Ebook, Inc.*
List Price: *$49.95*

The story of the man from La Mancha is more than just a tale of a man on a quest. It reaches deeper and reminds us of what it is to be human and to strive to attain that "impossible dream." Told in its entirety, the work has been faithfully translated by Magda Bogin and features an on-screen dictionary. This feature is good for building reading and vocabulary skills since it provides immediate and ready help (through hypertext links) with the meaning of some of the more difficult words in the text.

As with other titles in Ebook's *Multimedia Storybook* series, the text is fully narrated and the book can be set to "read" itself aloud. The user can follow along with the text displayed on the screen, or keep the narrative running in auto mode in the background while other tasks are performed in the foreground.

Forty-three excellent full-color illustrations by Manuel Boix illuminate the text and provide graphic interpretations of the story segments. To complete the multimedia experience, music by Joaquin Rodrigo is also an integral part of the disc.

A particularly nice feature of the disc is that the music and narration can be played on any stereo CD player, so the tale of Don Quixote can be enjoyed even when you're not using a PC with a CD-ROM drive.

Just as any well-rounded bookshelf would be incomplete without a print copy of this timeless work, every CD-ROM library should have a copy of this multimedia masterpiece as well.

CD-ROM REVIEW

Title: Electronic Library of Art, The
Format(s): MPC
Publisher: Ebook, Inc.
List Price: $79.95

The Electronic Library of Art is an extensive, enlightening window to the history of art, from primitive cave paintings to the most influential works of the twentieth century.

You can browse through thousands of full-color art images, indexed by artist, title, medium, school, and subject. You can study classical paintings, sculpture, and architecture. You can explore the Renaissance art of Italy, France, and Spain. And you will find it fascinating, educational, and entertaining all at the same time.

A detail function gives you a closer look at the focal points of most works, while electronic data cards provide illuminating facts, often accompanied by explanatory text and audio portions.

You'll learn how Monet, Cezanne, Renoir, and others exchanged ideas during the early exhibitions of Impressionism. You'll be able to compare and contrast the styles of Picasso, Chagall, and other Cubists. And with a few easy keystrokes, you can print biographical profiles which examine the social and economic factors that shaped the lives and styles of the masters to create your own essays and presentations complete with images.

This disc, one of Ebook's multivolume series products, puts the finest art images in the world right at your fingertips. This CD-ROM, a powerful resource for scholars, artists, students, and art lovers, makes a most welcome addition to any optical media library.

CD-ROM REVIEW

Title: Exotica-ROM
Format(s): PC and Mac
Publisher: Gazelle Technologies
List Price: $199.00

Anyone who's ever glanced the pages of *Playboy Magazine* or who was a devotee of the T.V. series *Beauty and the Beast* or has scanned the covers of magazines such as *Heavy Metal* has probably seen and admired the work of fantasy artist Olivia De Berardinis. Olivia's specialty is the representation of the female form with a dreamlike, erotic approach that is her signature. Her virtuosity includes works in pencil, gouache, pastel, acrylic, oils, and watercolors, utilizing brush and airbrush. Olivia's art is presented on the *Exotica-ROM*, which consists of over 200 of her works.

The disc is a hybrid, so it can be read by PCs or Macs. As a special bonus, Macintosh users can enjoy a QuickTime interview with the artist, which is also included on the latest version of this CD-ROM, version 3.0.

Viewer/browser programs are provided for previewing and displaying the images for both PCs and Macs. Multiple image formats are provided to give you just the right graphic treatment for your particular application, and these images can be imported into desktop publishing, word processing, graphics, and other applications. Macintosh formats include 24-bit and 8-bit color TIFF, 8-bit color PICT, grayscale PICT, grayscale TIFF, and MacPaint formats. PC-compatible formats include 24- and 8-bit color TIF, grayscale TIF, and color GIF.

This is a fine collection of erotic fantasy illustration.

CD-ROM REVIEW

Title: **Family Doctor, The**
Format(s): **MPC, PC and Mac**
Publisher: **Creative Multimedia Corporation**
List Price: **$79.99**

This new MPC incarnation of *The Family Doctor* adds enhanced information and an easy-to-use interface to CMC's best-selling home medical guide on CD-ROM.

The most significant feature of the MPC version is the illustrated human anatomy that provides three different views of five different body systems: muscular and skeletal, digestive, respiratory and circulatory, urinary and reproductive, and the nervous system. While viewing the illustrations the user can also call up voice-over pronunciations of 250 body systems and parts as well as supporting text explaining the significance of particular portions of the anatomy.

This new version also features updated information with almost 500 new items added to the Question and Answer section, giving advice on almost 2,000 of the most commonly asked health questions. Just under 300 color illustrations simplify the explanations, and a glossary of more than 100 medical terms provides valuable reference information. Other reference capabilities include comprehensive data on more than 1,600 prescription drugs as well as health update booklets and local and national resource listing and support groups.

The Family Doctor is based on the work of Dr. Allan Bruckheim, a physician, educator and the author of the Tribune Media's syndicated *Family Doctor* column. This is a hybrid disc that can be used with DOS, MPC, and Macintosh computers.

CD-ROM REVIEW

Title: Funny: The Movie in QuickTime
Format(s): Mac
Publisher: Warner New Media
List Price: $39.95

The content and point of this disc revolves around one central theme: eighty-four people were asked to tell the funniest joke or story they had ever heard. The result is a CD-ROM that contains the full-length, award-winning film "Funny," which plays right on your computer screen thanks to QuickTime.

QuickTime is an Apple system enhancement that makes simultaneous sound and video in real time possible on the Macintosh. You can watch the complete movie, or quickly find any moment in the film.

The movie itself features the video performances of nearly 100 jokes conveniently indexed by topic, length, tastefulness (or the lack of it), color of the comic's hair, and more. The performances appear in windows on the Mac's screen, and clicking on any window activates that segment. Fun topics and categories provide access to every joke in the film for those who like the "a la carte" approach.

The package warns that *Funny* contains something to offend all thinking, feeling life forms—gratuitous nudity, obscenity and off-color humor. If you can't take a joke, this CD-ROM is not for you. If you do possess a reasonably broad mind and a healthy sense of humor, however, you'll howl at much of the material on this disc. The jokesters include cab drivers, waitresses, Dick Cavett, the girl next door, and some surprise storytellers, too.

To run *Funny* you'll need a 13 inch color monitor, at least 4MB of RAM, a CD-ROM drive and a desire to laugh out loud.

CD-ROM REVIEW

Title: Goferwinkel's Adventures: The Lavender Land
Format(s): MPC
Publisher: Ebook, Inc.
List Price: $49.95

If you have a youngster in your household, or even if you're an adult who enjoys cartoons, then *Goferwinkel's Adventures* is a CD-ROM that's sure to please you.

Lavender Land can best be described as a multimedia comic book. Presented in traditional "panel" art form with the added touch of 256-color graphics, this multimedia comic book provides hours of enjoyment over and over again for kids of all ages.

The disc provides synchronized speech and text, music, animation, and a high level of interactivity with the user. The story line follows a classic-style fantasy with a technological twist that makes it a joy to view, hear and use.

Over twenty original drawings by Guy Boucher in 256-color palettes illuminate the work, while the voices of Hugh Corston and Suzanne Fortin provide the dialogue for the on-screen cartoon characters. The musical portions are fully orchestrated and realtime animation sequences add life and bounce to the story.

Goferwinkel, a spunky little bird, is set with the task of restoring peace and happiness in the Lavender Land as he tries to find his way home in this, his first adventure in this new series developed by MegaToon.

The CD-ROM is a charming piece of work with very high production standards, excellent content, and an entertaining story line that will amuse and entertain everyone in the household, particularly the younger set.

Title: *Great Literature*
Format(s): *PC and Mac*
Publisher: *Bureau Development, Inc.*
List Price: *$99.00*

Great Literature is a "must-have" CD-ROM that works on a Macintosh or IBM-compatible PC.

The full text of 1,896 literary classics with illustrations, CD-quality voice-overs and music performances comprise this chock-full CD-ROM. Famous narrations by Dave Coulier, Bob Saget and George Kennedy enliven many of the works, further augmented by live (not synthesized) musical performances. Full search and browse capability is provided for both images and text, so using the disc is easy.

There are too many titles to list here, but this gives you an abbreviated sampling of what's on Great Literature: Selected stories from *1,001 Nights, Aesop's Fables, Articles of the Constitution*, the *Constitution of the U.S.*, the *Declaration of Independence*, the *Emancipation Proclamation*, *Beowulf*, Emily Bronte's *Last Lines*, works by Lord Byron, Lewis Carroll, Cervantes, Chaucer's *Canterbury Tales*, the *Sayings of Confucius*, Dante's *Divine Comedy*, Darwin's *Origin of the Species*, *Grimm's Fairy Tales*, Martin Luther's *Ninety Five Theses*, Plato's *Apology*, Christopher Marlowe's *Dr. Faustus*, the poems of Edgar Allen Poe, Walt Whitman's poems, William Wordsworth's poems, and much more.

The user interface makes it easy to read, browse through this vast collection of books, and instantly search by word, event, book, picture, or article. This disc is a fantastic resource for libraries, schools, historians, students, and just about anyone else who enjoys great literature.

CD-ROM REVIEW

Title: Guinness Multimedia Disc of Records—1992
Format(s): PC
Publisher: Compton's New Media
List Price: $59.95

How would you like to hear the world's fastest talker? How about the world's fastest backwards talker? Would you like to hear native speakers pronounce the twelve longest words in twelve different languages including Japanese, Spanish, French, Croatian, and Italian? Are you interested in all kinds of arcane records for just about any kind of feat you could think of? If you answered "yes" to any or all of these questions, then the 1992 Edition of the *Guinness Multimedia Disc of Records* is sure to find favor with you.

The disc, compiled by Guinness Superlatives of Great Britain, features the text of over 7,000 world records. Additionally there are 300 high-resolution color pictures and approximately seventy animal, natural and historical sounds. Unlike the typical sound "bytes" found on other discs, these sounds are unique and include the rumble of an earthquake, the words of Neil Armstrong as he became the first man to set foot on the moon, and an authentic recording of the Ivory-Billed Woodpecker, a bird now believed to be extinct.

The interface is Compton's SmartTrieve software, which makes accessing the desired information easy and also affords excellent browsing possibilities as well.

As an added special bonus, the celebrity acceptance speeches from the thirty-third Annual Grammy Awards are also included on the disc. As a general reference work, or as an entertaining and recreational title, this disc is excellent.

CD-ROM REVIEW

Title: Info-Power
Format(s): PC
Publisher: Information USA, Inc.
List Price: $149.95

The United States Government is the largest consumer, generator, publisher, and repository of information on virtually every subject imaginable. Without exaggeration, if you need information on something—anything—chances are excellent that the Federal Government has volumes on it and it's usually free for the asking. But who to ask? Anyone who's ever had dealings with any branch of the government knows what a jungle of red-tape and bureaucracy it can be.

Info-Power by Matthew Lesko, the premiere pundit on how to get what the government gives away, provides a database of governmental agencies and a powerful search engine that supports Boolean operators to cut through the maze and help you zero-in on the government agency, it's address and phone number and contact person that can provide the information you need. What's more, in most cases this information is free (or close to it) and it's yours for a phone call or a letter to request it.

Info-Power is also available on floppy disk. The CD-ROM version includes the texts of Lesko's best-selling books (*Governmental Giveaways for Entrepreneurs*, the *Federal Database Finder* and *The Great American Gripe Book*), in addition to *Info-Power,* his latest title.

Regardless of what kind of information you need, the government probably has volumes on the subject waiting for someone to ask for it. *Info-Power* tells where and how to ask your Uncle Sam to be your research assistant.

Title: *Jazz: A Multimedia History*
Format(s): *MPC*
Publisher: *Compton's New Media*
List Price: *$99.95*

CD-ROM REVIEW

This disc, produced by Ebook and distributed through Compton's New Media, is a melodic journey that introduces you to the world of jazz music.

The disc is highly interactive and the user is encouraged to travel from the origins of jazz to the vibrant, electric sounds of today's contemporary jazz and fusion musical styles.

You'll be able to hear quotes and interviews from jazz musicians that give you interesting insights into what the jazz scene is all about. You'll be able to see how early jazz evolved into what it is today, and you'll learn how to interpret the nuances of jazz while enhancing your appreciation—without knowing music notation!

You'll learn about the inventors and the innovators of different styles like ragtime, swing, bebop, fusion, big band, and soul. This disc contains a complete chronology of the music and masters complete with photos, sound effects and jazz music from 1923 to 1991.

Duke Ellington, Charlie Parker, Louis Armstrong, and other founding fathers of jazz are biographied as well as contemporary musical innovators like Herbie Hancock, Miles Davis, and Weather Report. Ella Fitzgerald, Carmen McRae, Al Jarreau, Bobby McFerrin, and others are covered as well in this rich musical tapestry, and selected recordings from these artists are also included.

If you're a jazz aficionado, or just a music lover in general, *Jazz: A Multimedia History* hits a high note.

CD-ROM REVIEW

Title: KGB-CIA World Factbook
Format(s): PC
Publisher: Compton's New Media
List Price: $49.95

Let's face it—it's a big world out there and no one can be expected to know it all. That's why the KGB and the CIA (as well as other intelligence agencies around the world) compile and publish world "fact books" to keep their agents and operatives apprised of current political, economic and social climates for hundreds of locales around the world. Now you can have the inside info on such material as well.

Governmental and geographic statistics, political and diplomatic protocol, environmental and industrial issues, travel schedules and communication codes, trade traffic and drug traffic, world economics and currency conversions, the United Nations system, and world defense forces—all this and much, much more is covered on this fascinating disc.

The CD-ROM can be run from either DOS or Windows and features Compton's New Media *SmarTrieve* system, which permits you to look up information without leaving the application you're working in. To use the *SmarTrieve* functions, you merely hit a hot key and the software does the rest, jumping instantly to provide you with a list all references in the text which match your search. The *SmarTrieve* TSR works with all of Compton's titles using this technology, and it is an effective and easy means of accessing information fast.

Facts and figures for over 250 countries and territories worldwide are covered in this title, and it is updated yearly to keep the information current.

CD-ROM REVIEW

Title: *Klotski*
Format(s): PC
Publisher: *Quanta Press*
List Price: *$19.95*

The game of *Klotski* is based on an ancient Polish puzzle board game, and anyone who has enjoyed playing *Tetris* is a natural candidate for *Klotski* as well. The *Klotski* puzzles are really mathematical problems in block presentation that become more difficult as the player progresses through all fifty puzzles. The challenge level is progressive, so solving early puzzles is child's play in comparison to the more demanding upper levels.

A true Windows 3.1 application, *Klotski* utilizes a mouse for moving the puzzle pieces. Sound effects are provided to keep the game interesting on an audio plane as well. The game installs to the PC's hard drive so the CD-ROM isn't required for gameplay.

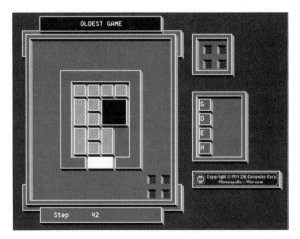

FIGURE 8.8 *The first of Klotski's 50 puzzle screens looks innocuous enough, but things get tough in a hurry as the level of difficulty increases with each new puzzle. The objective of this one is maneuver the dark-colored square around to get it through the opening at the bottom of the maze.*

CD-ROM REVIEW

Title: Library of the Future Series—Second Edition
Format(s): PC
Publisher: World Library, Inc.
List Price: $399.00

Imagine having over 2,000 separate pieces of literature, history, religion, science, philosophy, poetry, drama, government, and children's classics from over 950 titles on one CD-ROM—all at your fingertips and accessible in seconds. That's what you get with the *Library of the Future Series—Second Edition.*

The timeless classics of history's most renowned authors are now available to you and all 2,000 pieces are complete and unabridged.

World Library's Access Search and Retrieval software is among the best I've come across, and it allows you to search for specific words or phrases or you can search by era, country of origin, subject and more. For consumers it the most comprehensive, impressive and easiest-to-store library imaginable; for researchers, writers and students, it's like having 24-hour access to a good municipal library without having to leave your chair.

Some of the other noteworthy features about this disc are its ability to compare two works simultaneously (side by side), make reference notes within the text, set a bookmark, adjust the width of the screen for easier reading and preset the autoscroll feature to a comfortable reading speed. An illustration index has also been added to this edition which takes you to the pages of the original pictures, charts and maps, and allows you to advance into the text instantly from each of the more than 150 illustrations. This disc is truly a wealth of literature for everyone.

CD-ROM REVIEW

Title: LIFEmap Series
Format(s): Mac
Publisher: Warner New Media
List Price: $39.99 each

Do you know how life began? Or how insects learned to fly? Or what the dinosaur Tyrannosaurus rex and your Thanksgiving turkey have in common?

LIFEmap unravels the 3.5 billion-year-old history of life on Earth, starting at the very beginning of evolution.

A Macintosh II series or higher computer equipped with a 13-inch color monitor, at least 5MB of RAM and System Software 6.0.7 or later is required to run any of the three discs that comprise the LIFEmap series. The first disc in the series is titled *Organic Diversity* and it explores the worlds of bacteria, algae, fungi, and land plants. The second disc is *Animals with Backbones*, which is devoted to fish, amphibians, reptiles, and mammals. The third disc is *Animals*, and this CD-ROM deals with spiders, insects, mollusks, and sea stars.

There are over 1,000 screens detailing the wonders of evolution that provide a fascinating journey of discovery. *LIFEmap's* branching diagrams make it easy to chart your way through the evolutionary process. Developed by the research staff of the California Academy of Science in San Francisco as part of the exhibit Life Through Time, *LIFEmap* is the most comprehensive source of information about evolutionary relationships available in the world today.

With this disc, you control an information-rich multimedia environment of powerful graphics and special effects that unfolds the wondrous mysteries of life and evolution.

CD-ROM REVIEW

Title: Line and The Shape Eater, The
Format(s): MPC
Publisher: Cragsmoor Interactive
List Price: $39.95

This disc is an excellent adventure into learning and storytelling enhanced by multimedia interaction. *The Line and The Shape Eater*, by William Enco, introduces children to the basics of geometric shapes and shows the value of teamwork and cooperation. The importance of kindness toward others is stressed throughout the story line, and a choice of three narrators (including the author's 5-year-old son) is offered.

The Line is the central shape (or character) in the story, and The Line becomes a circle when it eats too much pie. Then the circle falls and becomes a square. On and on the story goes, showing children how simple shapes are basic parts of art, architecture and our world at large.

Along the way the evil Shape Eater comes to New York City. But, happily, different shapes throughout the city join together to help The Line transform The Shape Eater into a friendly creature.

The lesson taught therein is that shapes, like people, can be different and it is through cooperation and kindness that good comes about.

The child can interact with any of the shapes, too, or sit back to watch, listen, and learn from the narrator of his or her choice. A unique concept and means for teaching basic shape recognition as well as important social values, *The Line and Shape Eater* is a world of fun and learning for kids.

CD-ROM REVIEW

Title: **Lovely Ladies II**
Format(s): **PC**
Publisher: **HammerHead**
List Price: **$59.95**

HammerHead combined the best work of professional photographers with some of the best shareware software programs to present an easy and cost-effective way to look at stock photos. As the title of this disc suggests, the photographic subjects are indeed lovely ladies.

Lovely Ladies II contains 400 photographs by professional New York photographer, Bruce Curtis. His photos of these good-looking women have been scanned and organized on this CD-ROM to make it easier for you to see and use his photos in your work (usage rights are available). Of course, you can just enjoy this disc for the sake of viewing the beautiful models alone.

The images are in the Windows BMP format so they will work with all Windows applications. Each image comes in two sizes: 1024x768 (Super VGA) for photographic quality and 640x480 (VGA) for speedier viewing. For the "power user," the disc also contains ninety-four true-color (24-bit) images.

The subject matter is organized into four different categories: 111 pictures of models wearing fashion swimsuits, 113 pictures in lingerie, eighty-five pictures of women working out, and ninety-one close-ups of female body parts.

Five shareware programs for Windows 3.1 are also included on the disc: *Artshow, Paint Shop Pro, PixFolio, Wallman,* and *WinGIF.* These programs are for viewing, organizing, editing and manipulating the images on the disc.

This CD-ROM disc is, in a word, "lovely."

CD-ROM REVIEW

Title: Macmillan Dictionary for Children, The
Format(s): MPC
Publisher: Macmillan Electronic Publishing
List Price: $59.95

The *Macmillan Dictionary for Children* makes learning new words and their meanings fun.

The disc's friendly user interface is called Zak, an animated sprite who acts as your guide while using the dictionary.

Youngsters can start using the disc immediately by letting Zak take them on a personal tour of the dictionary, which is an entertaining way to learn about the disc's myriad features.

Content is certainly not lacking, with almost 12,000 word entries, 1,000 illustrations and 400 sounds effects. With some words a sound effect is played that reflects what the word means. You can also hear a spoken version of any word by clicking on its pronunciation icon. And to keep the child's interest level high, he or she can even join Zak in a game of hangman or a spelling bee.

Word entries can include definitions, sample sentences, pronunciations you can hear, illustrations, and sound effects. Help is a mere mouse-click away, and Zak can also be summoned at any time to give the introductory tour again if a refresher course is needed.

This disc is sure to provide hours of entertainment while it teaches vocabulary and language skills painlessly in the process. Macmillan's novel approach to introducing the dictionary is certain to attract and hold your child's attention. If you have a youngster in your house, this disc should be in your library.

Title: *Magiclips Music*
Format(s): *PC and Mac*
Publisher: *Wolfetone Multimedia Publishing*
List Price: *$89.95*

Wolfetone makes it practical and affordable to add high quality original production music to your multimedia applications and presentations.

Magiclips is professionally crafted original production music for computer, multimedia, film, and video presentations. The music is supplied in mixed-mode on the CD-ROM in formats that can be read by the computer and also played on an audio CD player.

The disc is designed to enable you to easily enhance your presentations with top-quality music in a variety of styles and lengths. "Que cards" are provided to help you locate just the sounds you want by *Feeling* (uptempo, inspirational, success), *Musical Style* (funky, jazzy, Caribbean), and Use (sports, product, travel). Fanfares, intros, outros, and beds, the essential building blocks of good production music, are all provided here.

You can use *Magiclips Music* on any number of presentations, sell as many as you like and publicly play or broadcast your presentations (including advertising uses) without paying any additional royalties or having to comply with any reporting requirements. Once you buy this disc, the music is yours to keep and use any way you desire.

Thirty-five *Magiclips Music* segments are provided in the following formats: 16-bit mono .WAV, 8-bit mono .WAV, 16-bit stereo .WAV, 8-bit mono .WAV (22kHz), 8-bit mono .WAV (11kHz), 8-bit mono .VOC (11kHz), and MIDI type 0, type 1, and Master Tracks Pro formats.

Title: Mammals: A Multimedia Encyclopedia
Format(s): PC
Publisher: National Geographic Society
List Price: $149.95

The National Geographic Society offers you a new multimedia tool for the home and school with this disc. The Society's updated, two-volume *Book of Mammals* expands into screen after screen of facts and fun. Mammals leap, dive, burrow, climb and fly. They even roar and bray and scream.

With just the click of a mouse, the world of mammals comes to life with: 700 full-screen photos, 150 range maps, 150 fact screens, 150 vital statistics screens, 155 authentic vocalizations, forty-five motion video clips from NGS's award-winning TV documentaries, and essays equivalent to more than 600 pages of text.

You also get a fact-packed caption with every photograph, a mammal classification game that makes learning fun and a pop-up glossary. Red Book audio permits playing sounds through the line-out or headphone jacks of the CD-ROM drive.

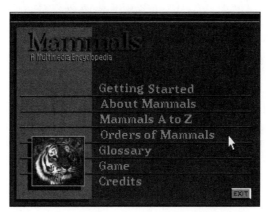

FIGURE 8.9 One of the first CD-ROMs to feature full-motion video and sound, Mammals is easy to use and a delight for the whole family.

CD-ROM
REVIEW

Title: Microsoft Bookshelf/1992
Format(s): MPC
Publisher: Microsoft Corporation
List Price: $199.95

Probably the most useful single CD-ROM produced for the vast majority of users, *Microsoft Bookshelf* has been improved and updated for 1992 and is now an MPC title to augment its cache of information with multimedia presentations.

This CD-ROM literally puts a full bookshelf's worth of standard reference works at your instantaneous disposal. And since all of the information is dynamically linked, you can jump at will from a main topical area to subordinate or ancillary areas of information should you desire more depth or detail.

The disc is chock-full of information including the entire text of the following works: *The Concise Columbia Encyclopedia* with 15,000 entries including maps, illustrations, and animations; *The American Heritage Dictionary* with more than 65,000 entries, each pronounced, and almost 1,000 illustrations; *Roget's II Electronic Thesaurus* with over 50,000 entries; *The World Almanac and Book of Facts 1992* with important facts and statistics about every nation in the world including the latest U.S. census data; *Bartlett's Familiar Quotations* with 22,500 quotations organized both chronologically and by the author's name; *Hammond Atlas* with maps of countries worldwide; and all fifty of the United States plus national flags and anthems.

Multimedia animations bring complex ideas to life and make understanding them easier. Regardless of whether you use your MPC system at home, in business or at school, you'll find *Microsoft Bookshelf/1992* to be almost as indispensable as your mouse.

Title: *Microsoft Cinemania*
Format(s): *MPC*
Publisher: *Microsoft Corporation*
List Price: *$99.95*

Microsoft Cinemania is an MPC interactive movie guide. Regardless of what type of information you desire on cinema, filmmaking or people in the movie industry, chances are excellent you'll find it on this disc.

As a source of cinema critique, over 19,000 capsule reviews from *Leonard Maltin's Movie and Video Guide 1992* are included as well as in-depth reviews of 500 selected and 245 recent films.

If its people you're interested in, the disc also contains information on over 3,000 movie personalities including stars, key executive and production personnel, character actors and Academy Award winners.

Over 1,000 photos are also included that provide a look at famous movie scenes or portraits of the actors appearing in them. Dialogue "sound bytes" from selected films are also included, but an MPC-compliant PC is required to take advantage of all this disc has to offer.

A comprehensive glossary of cinematography terminology is provided to define "best boy," "gaffer," "post-production," and more.

Finding the information is easy since the disc runs under Windows and provides a full GUI. You can select films, genres, actors or other "screening" criteria to produce lists of films which meet your specifications before you set out to the video store. This disc is an excellent resource as well as a highly entertaining product.

CD-ROM REVIEW

Title: **Microsoft Musical Instruments**

Format(s): **MPC**

Publisher: **Microsoft Corporation**

List Price: **$99.95**

More than 200 musical instruments from all around the world come to life in *Microsoft Musical Instruments,* an MPC CD-ROM which is a real treat for anyone who loves music.

Articles are provided on each instrument that explore the history of the instrument while providing over 500 excellent photographs and 1,500 sound samples.

Familiar instruments as well as exotic ones from the farthest reaches of the globe—everything from accordion to zurna—are covered in great depth and detail. You can zoom-in on information with a click of the mouse or jump from one section of the program to another, since all of the data is dynamically linked.

In the *Instruments of the World* section of the disc you can invoke a regional display of instruments from different areas of the world along with sound samples of each. Clicking on an instrument brings forth a full-page article.

The *Musical Ensembles* portion provides sound samples of different musical styles (chamber music to steel drums and everything in between) for listening and learning. The sound samples are full-fidelity recordings of professional musicians using the actual instruments.

Based on the highly acclaimed *Eyewitness Guide* book series, this disc takes you on a wonderfully interactive tour of music and the instruments that make it all around the world. It is excellent for anyone of any age.

Title: *Mother Earth II*
Format(s): *PC*
Publisher: *HammerHead*
List Price: *$59.95*

Need a photo for a magazine article or advertisement? Try out a couple of photos you like—on the computer screen—with your text in place. Experiment with different pictures for that presentation or newsletter project you're working on. Selecting stock photography has never been easier than it is with CD-ROM.

Mother Earth II contains 460 photographs by professional New York photographer Bruce Curtis. Curtis travels the world to capture what he sees on film, and his photos were scanned and placed on this CD-ROM. Each picture is supplied in two different sizes: high resolution 1024x768 (Super VGA) for photographic quality and standard resolution 640x480 (VGA) for faster selection viewing.

As the disc's title suggests, the subject matter is about the wonders of the natural world. 460 bitmap (BMP) images of ocean horizons, awesome sunsets, sun-drenched beaches and the heart-warming New England countryside provide myriad possibilities for use in any Windows application including word processors, spreadsheets, painting programs, and all kinds of graphics and photo-editing programs.

A suite of shareware applications that help you organize, categorize, edit, and print every one of the 460 images is also included. And since these applications are shareware, you only pay for what you use and you know if you like it before you pay for it. The images can also be viewed, edited, and manipulated with any other software that can handle the BMP format as well.

Title: **MPC Wizard**
Format(s): **MPC**
Publisher: **Aris Entertainment**
List Price: **$14.95**

CD-ROM REVIEW

Without a doubt, *MPC Wizard* is one of the biggest CD-ROM bargains available for every Windows user, especially those who are into multimedia.

The *MPC Wizard* is a test and tune-up CD-ROM disc for Windows that contains diagnostic tests to check your VGA and CD-ROM performance, tune your sound card and give you tips to maximize your multimedia PC.

Hundreds of the latest drivers for video and sound cards are also included on the disc, along with an easy-to-use interface for running the tests, installing drivers, or troubleshooting.

In addition to all of the above, a generous sampling of Aris' *Media Clips* is also included. A collection of fifty images and fifty sounds that can be used for presentations, education or fun—royalty free! If you're looking for a CD-ROM bargain, this is it!

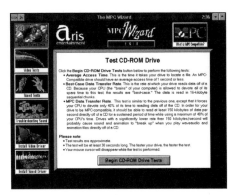

FIGURE 8.10 The MPC Wizard from Aris Entertainment contains hundreds of Windows video and sound drivers, tests, and utilities in addition to a generous sampling of Media Clips from Aris' other CD-ROM titles.

Title: *Murder Makes Strange Deadfellows*
Format(s): *PC and MPC*
Publisher: *Tiger Media*
List Price: *$49.95*

Looking for an adventure you can get your teeth into? One that has murder, mayhem, ghosts, ghouls, goblins, and plots aplenty? Walk this way, if you dare!

The second multimedia title in the award-winning *Airwave Adventure* series, *Murder Makes Strange Deadfellows* proves that death is no laughing matter. The main story line goes like this: Randolph Steere, powerful patriarch of the Steere family, has died in a fall. Family, friends and associates have gathered at Steere Manor to find out what Randolph left them—if, in fact, he left them anything at all!

Your task is to guide Randolph's young nephew Nick through the foreboding mansion where this world and the next collide head-on with hilariously terrifying results. Was Randolph's death an accident. Is his last Will his last word? Is Steere Manor really alive with dead people. Find out for yourself with this disc—it's sure to keep you occupied for many, many hours.

In addition to absolutely superb graphics and excellent production values throughout the program, the accompanying music is first-rate as well. Track 1 on this CD-ROM contains all of the computer data, so it should not be played through a pair of speakers. The remainder of the tracks, however, are standard Red Book Audio and, as such, are playable on any audio CD player. Be sure to note that a SoundBlaster or ThunderBoard audio card is required to play the DOS version of *Murder Makes Strange Deadfellows* and multimedia-capable hardware for the MPC version.

CD-ROM REVIEW

Title: **Murmurs of Earth**
Format(s): **PC and Mac**
Publisher: **Warner New Media**
List Price: **$59.99**

If you're a native of this planet (and I presume that includes the majority of readers if not all of you!), then you will be interested in *Murmurs of Earth*, the Voyager Interstellar Record.

A hybrid disc that works on a Macintosh or IBM-compatible PC, the CD-ROM includes all 116 color images included in the Voyager Record.

This is a two-disc set that features all 90 minutes of the sound and music included in the Voyager Record, and both discs are playable on any CD player.

In addition to the two-disc set, a printed booklet is also provided which contains a complete track listing of all audio and visual selections, plus an update on the progress and significance of Voyager.

Track 1 of the first disc contains computer data that is not intended for audio playback and can possibly cause damage to audio equipment if played. Tracks 2 to 4 contain greetings from the peoples of Earth, while track 5 contains the sounds of earth. Tracks 6 to 16 contain music, and disc two contains music only on all sixteen tracks.

The graphic content of this disc is profound in its inherent simplicity and symbolism that, hopefully, conveys a non-threatening message of "hello" to whatever sentient lifeforms the Voyager encounters as it continues its journey where no man—or anything else from Earth, for that matter—has gone before.

CD-ROM REVIEW

Title: **Nautilus Monthly Magazine**
Format(s): **MPC and Mac**
Publisher: **Metatec/Discovery Systems**
List Price: **$9.95/issue**

Nautilus is a multimedia magazine published monthly on CD-ROM that provides information and software for Macintosh and PC/Windows users.

The content of *Nautilus* varies with each issue, but generally runs the gamut from utilities to programming tools to games and newly released CD audio tracks. A typical issue might contain a collection of the best shareware and commercial demos, commentary and industry news, tech tips and tools, teachers' resources and educational programs, multimedia presentations and "building blocks" such as photos, graphics and clip art, sound effects and production music, MIDI files, and desktop publishing components and tutorials.

Separate issues are published for Macintosh and PC users, thus providing the best material for both formats on a monthly disc dedicated to each machine format.

An annual (12-issue) subscription in North America is $137.40, which breaks down to $9.95 per issue plus $1.50 for shipping and handling. Metatec/Discovery Systems also has a "pay as you go" subscription option available as well.

A sample *Nautilus* disc is available for a shipping and handling charge of $4.95, and a three-disc "mini-subscription" (the *Intro to Nautilus* plus two regular issue discs) is also available at a suggested retail price of $29.95 if you'd like to try *Nautilus* on a trial basis. Every issue is loaded with lots of helpful information, reviews and other items which make it worthwhile.

Be sure to see the Nautilus coupon offer at the end of this book.

CD-ROM REVIEW

Title: New Basics Electronic Cookbook, The
Format(s): PC
Publisher: Xiphias
List Price: $69.95

Created from the best-selling *Silver Palate Cookbook* series by authors Julee Rosso and Sheila Lukins, *The New Basics Electronic Cookbook* includes a library of over 1,800 delicious recipes, hundreds of colorful pictures and a whole range of helpful cooking hints, spoken by the authors themselves!

The audio portions of the disc play through the CD-ROM drive's headphone or line output jacks, so there's no need to have a sound board installed in the PC to use this disc.

You can pick the search parameters from food groups, custom menus or meal types. If you want to substitute ingredients, change portions or switch to metric, the tools to do so are readily available.

The data is rich with "hot word" hypertext links that instantly provide supplemental information and a complete inventory of ingredient pictures makes food selection easy.

This multimedia cookbook is rich with helpful information on buying, preparing and serving delicious meals. It can help you design a gourmet menu using ingredients that are already at hand, making it the kitchen reference of tomorrow for today's creative cook. With this disc, some basic culinary ingredients and a little effort you'll be producing gastronomic delights aplenty!

In addition to the DOS version, Xiphias has also released this title in formats for Commodore CDTV, Tandy/Memorex VIS, and the Sony Data Discman. These formats each carry a suggested list price of $59.95 each.

Title: *New Grolier Multimedia Encyclopedia*
Format(s): *MPC*
Publisher: *Grolier Electronic Publishing*
List Price: *$395.00*

The multimedia aspects of this encyclopedia are what sets it apart from all of the other CD-ROM-based encyclopedias I've included here.

Video for Windows technology makes it possible to view motion video clips of historical events, famous people in history, NASA missions, major sporting events and more, and that's exactly what you'll find on this outstanding disc.

It is the addition of Video for Windows technology that makes this the best edition yet of Grolier's CD-ROM-based encyclopedia which comprises the 10-million-word text and many of the pictures from Grolier's 21-volume *Academic American Encyclopedia.* Some of the other new features added to this MPC version include animated sequences of aircraft technology, weather, the human body, the solar system, and more. Some of the many video clips include the Hindenberg disaster, John Kennedy's inaugural speech, JFK's "put a man on the moon" speech, Richard Nixon's resignation speech, Lindberg's flight, the moon landing, Hitler, and much, much more. Many of the videos are accompanied by sound, making this a remarkable multimedia experience—this disc gives little snippet's of history you can recall any time you desire.

Thousands of color and black-and-white pictures including over 1,000 new pictures for this edition and more than 250 high-resolution color maps make this one of the most information-packed CD-ROMs you can get. A multimedia-capable PC is required to take full advantage of all the features of this disc.

CD-ROM REVIEW

Title: Phethean's Public Domain #2
Format(s): PC
Publisher: Peter J. Phethean, Ltd.
List Price: $99.00

It is quite possible that it will take you days, weeks—even months—to thoroughly go through all of the data this chock-full CD-ROM contains. There are almost 720 megabytes of public domain and shareware software on this disc.

13,371 files contained in 116 directories occupying 715,572,066 bytes of space run the gamut of subject matter and virtually ensure that there's something here for everyone, no matter what their interests may be.

In addition to the shareware and public domain software some copyrighted programs are also provided. Most of these reside in a subdirectory called CDTESTS that, as the name implies, contains performance-related utilities for your CD-ROM drive.

Programs on the disc range from keyboard, screen, disk caching, and other hardware-oriented programs and utilities to modem software, printer utilities, virus detection/removal programs, Windows applications, icons and bitmaps, programming utilities and libraries for BASIC, C, Pascal, Assembler, and more, loads of games, sound/voice files, word processing, desktop publishing, spreadsheet, science and engineering programs, CAD and CAM files, food and recipes, health files, kid stuff, humor, Ham radio, Bible and church, and much, much more.

The user interface is easy to use, and all of the files are provided in compressed format to conserve space. The viewing and decompression software is also provided, so you can examine the applications before downloading them to your hard disk.

CD-ROM REVIEW

Title: Prescription Drugs
Format(s): PC and Mac
Publisher: Quanta Press
List Price: $79.95

This disc describes, in non-technical terms, the 200 most prescribed medications in the U.S., and it was developed to provide a collection of selected information not normally available from one source. The information about these drugs is totally text-based and was collected from standard drug reference manuals, government publications, drug manufacturer publications, and other sources. The information was edited, rewritten, amplified, and reorganized to provide an easy-to-read synopsis of the reference data available on each product.

Please note that this CD-ROM is for reference purposes only and is not intended to prevent or preclude the user from seeking the necessary medical, dental, nursing, or pharmacy advice for the treatment and control of disease. It is an excellent resource for gaining general information on today's most-prescribed drugs.

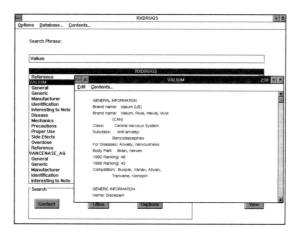

FIGURE 8.11 All data in Prescription Drugs is text-based and can be accessed by either typing in a key search word or using the pull-down menus to select the desired information category.

CD-ROM REVIEW

Title: *Presidents: It All Started With George, The*
Format(s): *PC*
Publisher: *National Geographic Society*
List Price: *$149.95*

This interactive CD-ROM features more than 1,000 captioned, full-screen photographs in VGA format, thirty-three video clips of significant historical moments, a multimedia timeline, famous speeches, narrated photo essays, a trivia game, political party index, a pop-up glossary, election facts, figures and maps, and personal glimpses of each president from George Washington to George Bush and every Chief Executive in between.

In order to access the audio portions of the program, audio support programs are provided for the IBM PS/2 M-Audio Capture and Playback adapter, IBM PS/1 audio/joystick adapter, Digispeech DS201 sound module, and the SoundBlaster audio board. An IBM PS/1, PS/2 or 100 percent IBM-compatible PC with 640K and VGA graphics adapter, a mouse and a CD-ROM drive completes the list of required hardware.

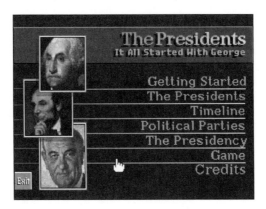

FIGURE 8.12 National Geographic makes learning about the men who have governed our country in its highest office fun, entertaining, and easy.

CD-ROM REVIEW

Title: *Private Pictures I*
Format(s): PC
Publisher: *Starware Publishing*
List Price: $99.95

CD-ROM provides something for every taste, even if that taste runs into the X-rated category.

Private Pictures I is a disc intended for adults only and is full of highly explicit, erotic subject matter. The CD-ROM contains over 600 color images and seventy mini-movies. The images are in a 256-color GIF format and most images have a sharp resolution of 640x480 pixels. It is important to note that these movies are not animations and are quite graphic in what they depict.

The VGA movies are actual captures that originate as live action video. Some of the movies are their own productions with action lasting up to five minutes, while others are simply a few repeating frames. All of the movies are in GL, DL, or FLI formats and include their appropriate viewers.

The interface for using the disc is provided by a menu utility which presents the various sections and programs on the disc for your selection. Virtually all of the menu selections merely require highlighting the desired selection with the cursor keys and pressing the enter key to begin the presentation. Also included on the CD-ROM is the Graphix Starter Kit software, which is a collection of shareware utilities for DOS and Windows, and there's even a menu option that installs the shareware on your hard drive if desired.

Private Pictures I is definitely not for the weak-hearted and may be considered offensive by some viewers. But for those desiring X-rated material, this disc is a real find.

CD-ROM REVIEW

Title: Seventh (7th) Wonder CD-ROM
Format(s): Mac
Publisher: Educorp
List Price: $59.95

This CD-ROM contains a collection of essential tools and utilities that will enhance your Macintosh. It has over 100MB of the most up-to-date System 7 specific public domain and shareware software available today. Included are the best of sounds, utilities, folder icons, "drag and drops," Power Book programs, communication tools, compression programs, extensions, finder tools, QuickTime movies, screen savers, security programs, virus utilities, TrueType fonts, *plus* System 7.0.1!

Here's a brief run-down of the content that makes this disc a super bargain for Mac users: over 175 double-clickable System 7 sounds, a myriad of useful utilities, and over 350 separate color folder icons ready to copy-and-paste directly to your folders.

There are also lots of QuickTime movies along with a variety of tools that allow you to edit and manipulate QuickTime movies. If you like screen savers you'll find a rich assortment of them here as well, including a variety of After Dark modules. Security programs for files, folders, floppy and hard discs are also included as well as virus utilities including the newly updated Disinfectant 2.9. And to give your word processing, desktop publishing, and presentation projects that professional touch over 120 TrueType fonts are also included on this disc.

The user interface is marvelously easy to use, and regardless of whether you're a Macintosh power user or just someone who enjoys exploring new ground with the Macintosh, you're bound to find lots of interesting things here.

CD-ROM REVIEW

Title: Software Jukebox
Format(s): PC
Publisher: Compton's New Media
List Price: $49.95

Three chart-topping games of fun and skill headline the *Software Jukebox* CD-ROM, but there's lots more included in the way of "test rides" of over fifty other great programs as well.

Links, the definitive golf game, provides the player with the Torrey Pines Golf Course reproduced in exacting detail, instant replays, incredible 3-D contoured terrain, three levels of gameplay, actual digitized trees and buildings, and all the sounds of true golf—from commentary on the plays to wildlife sounds to the sound of your swing as your club cuts through the air.

If golf is too tame for your tastes or you just want to get away from it all for a while, climb into the cockpit of *Jet Fighter* and fly the deadly skies. You choose the plane from a selection of an F-14 Tomcat, F-16 Fighting Falcon, or F/A-18 Hornet, and all of them are equipped with cutting-edge weaponry. You can get white knuckles flying over thirty intense missions with hostile MIG encounters augmented by the deadly threat of Silkworm missiles homing in on you for the kill.

Faces builds on the basic concept of *Tetris* but adds parts of the skull to give things a "fresh face" (excuse the pun). An import from the Soviet Union, *Faces* utilizes falling blocks that have pieces of famous (and not-so-famous) faces that must be stacked in the proper order to form complete faces. For crowd-pleasing fun, up to ten players can play head-to-head or in tournament modes. Fascinating fun for all here.

Title: *Sports Illustrated CD-ROM Sports Almanac*
Format(s): *Mac*
Publisher: *Warner New Media*
List Price: *$59.99*

Whether you're a jock or just a sports fan you'll love this disc from the creators of *Sports Illustrated,* America's most trusted sports magazine, now available on CD-ROM through Warner New Media.

Close to 10,000 sports facts and figures are now accessible with a single mouse click. This is an electronic reference guide of sports statistics and stories.

Your rotisserie picks will never be easier. Your game-time bets never more quickly settled. For example, just type in "Michael Jordan" to see the NBA's all-time highest regular scoring average, not to mention every additional statistic linked with "Air."

Magic Johnson, Monica Seles, Darryl Strawberry, John Daly, Thurman Thomas—these are just a few of the stars portrayed in the information-rich articles and sound-captioned photographs that put you in the middle of the action.

Noteworthy features of the disc include a chronological listing of the year's sports highlights, profiles of nearly 500 winning names in sports and a listing of athletic awards for every sport over the past 50 years.

A special bonus features is the Sports Market report. This is an inside look at the business of sports, including a directory of teams. So whether you actually participate in athletics or you're just an armchair athlete, you'll find the *Sports Almanac on CD-ROM* to be a sure hit.

CD-ROM REVIEW

Title: Sports ROM, The
Format(s): PC and Mac
Publisher: Gazelle Technologies
List Price: $69.95

If you're looking for a sports-oriented clip art collection, your search is over with *The Sports ROM*.

The sports activities covered include archery, badminton, baseball, basketball, fencing, football, Frisbee, golf, gymnastics, ping pong, racing, rugby, soccer, team handball, tennis, track and field, volleyball, and wrestling. Regardless of the sport, chances are excellent that there will be one or more high-quality illustration on the subject. For example, under "badminton," four illustrations are available: a male player smashing, a female stretching, a female posed, and a male looking up.

The images are provided in the popular TIFF image format, which is compatible with the majority of desktop publishing, art, graphics, and word processing programs. Outstanding detail assures excellent reproduction at virtually any size. This is a hybrid disc so it can be read by Macintoshes and IBM-compatible PCs.

FIGURE 8.13 This highly-detailed illustration of an Indy car is representative of the outstanding sports-oriented artwork in TIFF format for Macs and PCs on The Sports ROM.

CD-ROM REVIEW

Title: Talking Jungle Safari
Format(s): PC
Publisher: New Media Schoolhouse
List Price: $99.00

Talking Jungle Safari is an exciting and educational adventure for users of all ages (even preschoolers) who choose to venture through the African Jungle on this optical-media safari.

The disc enables users to see and hear the names of over eighty plants and animals in four different habitats: plains, rain forest, tall grass, and river front. Each of these sections begins with an animated travel sequence in which the user takes a jeep, helicopter, or riverboat to seek out the native wildlife indigenous to that locale.

The user interface is entirely graphical in nature, requiring only a mouse click to make a selection. Using the mouse, the user can see the animal's baby offspring, hear the name of the animal and read or listen to the fascinating facts about the animal. Even pre-readers can easily run and learn from this program, since all of the textual information is fully narrated in a clear, digitized human voice.

The audio portion of this disc utilizes standard Red Book Audio, which means that it plays through the CD-ROM drive's headphone or line-out jacks rather than relying on a sound board for playback.

A printing option is also provided to enable outputting "photographs" of the safari, and lifelike jungle sound effects accompany the narratives. Kids of all ages will love learning about the creatures of Africa with this excellent disc.

CD-ROM REVIEW

Title: Talking Schoolhouse CD
Format(s): PC
Publisher: New Media Schoolhouse
List Price: $99.00

Imagine one CD-ROM that incorporates five educational software titles into a complete learning experience and that's what you get with the *Talking Schoolhouse CD.*

This disc is the result of the latest techniques for teaching all of the basic skills. The program is an in-depth study of reading, spelling, mathematics, speech, and telling time for youngsters. The five complete programs can keep any child engaged for hours while making learning more fun than ever before.

The graphical user interface makes using the program a simple matter of pointing and shooting to explore all of the educational aspects of the program material. Preschoolers won't have any problem or compunction about using the program, thanks to interesting sound effects, lively graphics and vivid colors. Even pre-readers can easily run and learn from this program, since all of the textual information is fully narrated in a clear, digitized human voice. The interface is very easy to use and only requires pointing and clicking with a mouse to access all of the program's features.

The programs teach children map skills, word association, pronunciation, nouns, verbs, how to tell time, numbers, addition, subtraction, animal sounds, and basic computer skills—quite a package, indeed! This disc's audio plays through the CD-ROM drive's headphone or line-out jacks, so a sound card isn't required for playback.

This disc is great for any youngster.

CD-ROM REVIEW

Title: *Time Table of History Series*
Format(s): *PC*
Publisher: *Xiphias*
List Price: *$69.95 each*

Designed to be enjoyed by the entire family, there are currently three titles in the series, with more planned:

The Time Table of Science and Innovation is a journey through history from the Big Bang through the latest developments in U.S. military technology. Enhanced by special multimedia effects, the disc contains hundreds of pictures, graphics and maps, a prehistoric timeline, the periodic table and more. This disc is also available for the Macintosh, CDTV, and VIS at $69.95 per version, and for the Sony Data Discman at $39.95.

The Time Table of Business, Politics, and Media spans the period from the Trojan Horse through Desert Storm, covers business from the Persian Traders to Microsoft, and communication from the Pony Express to CNN. This original literary work is packed with over 6,400 stories enriched by hundreds of images, quotes, maps and more. This disc is also available in formats for the CDTV and VIS at $69.95 each and for the Sony Data Discman at $39.95.

The Time Table of Arts and Entertainment is the latest addition to the Time Table Series and contains over 4,200 original stories that start with the first cave paintings and finish with today's computerized choreography and animation. Multimedia effects include museum references, pictures, portraits, quotes and even music from some of the world's greatest composers. Versions are also available for CDTV and VIS at $69.95 per format and for the Sony Data Discman at $39.95.

CD-ROM REVIEW

Title: Total Baseball
Format(s): PC and Mac
Publisher: Creative Multimedia Corporation
List Price: $49.95

Total Baseball, edited by John Thorn and Pete Palmer, has been called the most comprehensive baseball reference ever compiled. With the power of the personal computer to process the massive amounts of data this CD-ROM contains, you can retrieve virtually any type of statistic, record or fact about the sport of baseball in a matter of seconds. In addition to all of this textual data, the disc also has audio sound bytes as well as photos and images.

This disc is a complete baseball library from 1871 to the 1991 World Series. It contains over 500 images of players, teams and ballparks, sound clips from some of baseball's most memorable moments and over 2,600 pages of text. You'll find the statistics of over 13,000 players, the batting, pitching and fielding registers for all Major League players, the top 100 all-time, life-time and single season leaders in all categories and more. The recipients of the MVP, Cy Young, and Rookie of the Year and Hall of Fame Awards. Full team rosters (including players, managers and owners) are also included.

This CD-ROM uses DiscPassage retrieval software, which is among the easiest to use interfaces for text-based material. From the various pull-down menus, you can search, browse, view, or hear the different kinds of data contained on this disc. Detailed articles on a variety of subjects from baseball streaks and feats to scandals and controversies are also included to make this a baseball lover's delight.

CD-ROM REVIEW

Title: **Twelve Roads to Gettysburg**
Format(s): **MPC**
Publisher: **Ebook, Inc.**
List Price: **$69.95**

While there are many works available on the Civil War both in print as well as in electronic format, this CD-ROM deals with the greatest battle fought in North America, which was also the turning point of the war: the Battle at Gettysburg. This battle was not only one of the decisive points of U.S. history, but it was an event so monumental that it is difficult to understand today, more than a century later. This disc does much to provide insight and dispel the fog of mystery surrounding the event.

Twelve Roads to Gettysburg tells the story in a way not available in any single textbook, any movie or in any single reference study. This truly unique illustrated multimedia CD-ROM tells its story using animation, photographs, period engravings, text, actual period music, and original narration.

With this disc you can follow the daily maneuvering of the armies as well as the politicians. Return to the times through many military terms and over 200 biographical sketches and historical data. Photos bring the faces and names in history books to life, while detailed information on both armies gives new insight to who the soldiers were, what they wore and ate, how many survived and even what happened to them.

To provide contrast, you're invited to compare the Gettysburg of yesterday with the Gettysburg of today. Step back through time and discover for yourself what happened between Generals Meade and Lee that shaped our country's destiny. This disc requires MPC hardware for proper playback of all portions.

CD-ROM REVIEW

Title: Ultima Underworld/Wing Commander II
Format(s): PC
Publisher: Origin Systems
List Price: $99.95

Origin Systems has taken two of its most successful titles and put them in their original, uncut versions together on one CD-ROM for IBM-compatible PCs (a SoundBlaster-compatible audio card is required for digitized speech and an AdLib, SoundBlaster or Roland-compatible sound card is required for music).

In *Ultima Underworld* you'll step into the first continuous-movement, first-person 3D dungeon, The Stygian Abyss, in this action fantasy adventure. You'll walk, run, swim and jump through 25 miles of sheer terror, casting spells, vanquishing foes and solving puzzles as you race to rescue the baron's kidnapped daughter.

The player's perspective is that of actually being "in" the game. You can look down on objects at your feet, or up to see creatures hovering overhead—every wall, precipice, object, and character has been painstakingly modeled in 3D space to impart a sense of realism that is augmented by the lush 256-color VGA graphics and a full, orchestral score. It's another world!

In *Wing Commander II* you'll have to prove yourself through forty-seven desperate missions which pick up where the original *Wing Commander* game left off. The game scenario has you transferred to a backwater outpost after a court martial, and you must earn the respect of the High Command and prevent the destruction of the Terran homeworlds. To do this you have to dogfight your way through a realistic universe created with the latest 3D rendering technology. It's an exciting, action packed game.

CD-ROM REVIEW

Title: U.S.A. Factbook
Format(s): PC and Mac
Publisher: Quanta Press
List Price: $49.95

How much do you know about the state you live in? Would you like to know more? If you answered "yes" to the last question, then this disc is for you.

The *U.S.A. Factbook* is an electronic almanac of the fifty United States and its territories. The disc is updated annually by Quanta and it includes extensive examinations of state geography, vital statistics (people), government and politics, economics, lines of communication, transportation, icons, traditions and other state and territory-specific information.

This disc is a full text search-and-retrieval database with images. Six-hundred-dot-per-inch TIF and PCX images are provided for maps and state seals. These images are viewable in the database and can also be downloaded to most desktop publishing systems.

A Hypercard stack is provided on a 3.5 inch floppy diskette for quick Macintosh search and retrieval.

Learn more about the U.S.A. with this excellent disc—it's the fun way to do it!

CD-ROM REVIEW

Title: U.S.A. Wars: Desert Storm
Format(s): PC
Publisher: Compton's New Media
List Price: $149.95

What were the primary targets of the first U.S. air sorties? What convinced General Schwarzkopf that it was time to launch a ground attack? What would you have done differently had *you* been in command? You'll be able to answer all of these questions and more if you have a copy of Compton's *U.S.A. Wars: Desert Storm* in your CD-ROM library.

The disc, which runs from DOS or Windows, includes the final report on the war by the U.S. Department of Defense. The battlefield comes to life through text, full-color VGA images, computer animation and sound. This CD-ROM can literally make you an expert on the subject of the Persian Gulf War.

You can find specific topics such as high-tech weaponry, planes and vehicles used during the conflict, as well as detailed diagrams and specifications. The transition from operation Desert Shield to Desert Storm is covered in depth and detail and text and graphics can be printed or exported to help you create your own custom, in-depth reports.

A special bonus is the inclusion of the Coalition Command DataGame, an educational, interactive program that puts you in command of the U.S. forces and permits you to set policies for providing information to the media, gives you vital feedback through direct "hotlines" to the White House and Pentagon and empowers you to deploy air and ground forces from a sophisticated command post. The disc uses Compton's SmarTrieve TSR software, so you can invoke the program from within another application.

**CD-ROM
REVIEW**

Title: **U.S. History on CD-ROM**
Format(s): **PC and Mac**
Publisher: **Bureau Development, Inc.**
List Price: **$395.00**

Awarded the 1991 Optical Publishing Association award for the Best Education Product, this CD-ROM contains the full text of 107 books relating to U.S. History, from the arrival of the Native Americans to the present time. Detailed coverage from a variety of historical perspectives of U.S. political, social, military, and economic history is provided, and the disc includes over 1,000 beautiful VGA photos, maps, and tables of historical events. Since this CD-ROM is a hybrid disc, it can be used on either a Macintosh or an IBM-compatible PC without a problem.

A simple user interface makes it easy to browse through this vast collection of history books, print articles or stories, and instantly search by word, event, book, picture, or article. This disc makes a fantastic resource for libraries, schools, historians, government officials, students, or just about anyone else who understands the importance of today's history and how it pertains to tomorrow's events.

A sampling of some of the 107 titles includes *American Home Front, Black Americans, Criminal Justice, Iran-Contra Affair* (three volumes), *NASA: The First 25 Years, Presidential Proclamations, Fords Theatre, Mount St. Helens, Our Country* (eight volumes), *Watergate/Nixon Transcripts, Pearl Harbor,* and much, much more.

For classroom and group uses, network versions are also available. The two to nine user network version carries a list price of $995, while the network version for ten or more users lists at $1,995.

CD-ROM REVIEW

Title: U.S. Presidents
Format(s): PC and Mac
Publisher: Quanta Press
List Price: $69.95

U.S. Presidents is a comprehensive resource of facts about the forty-one men who served in our nation's highest office. (Updates will be issued to include Bill Clinton, who has not yet been inaugurated as of this writing.)

Information is provided in matters presidential, including the date the president was born, the city of his birth, his family background and ancestry, the first ladies and presidential children, the president's religion, dates of the president's term in office, major events that occurred during the president's term, political parties and affiliations, the vice-presidents, the cause of death, date and circumstances surrounding the president's death, and much more.

There are loads of interesting historical and presidential facts including the answers to such questions as: "who formed the Bull Moose party," "what president was nicknamed the 'little magician'," "how many assassination attempts have been made on U.S. Presidents," and other fascinating facts about those who have commanded from the Oval Office.

In addition to a wealth of textual information which is easily retrieved with the supplied interface, the disc also contains full-color VGA and Super VGA portraits of the presidents.

The disc is a hybrid, so it can be used on both Macintosh and IBM-compatible PCs. Any American interested in the individuals who have held this office should buy this CD-ROM.

CD-ROM REVIEW

Title: Where in the World is Carmen Sandiego/Deluxe
Format(s): PC
Publisher: Broderbund
List Price: $99.95

This award-winning game, a long-time favorite on magnetic media, is now available in an enhanced Deluxe Edition on CD-ROM.

The game turns geography into an exciting world-wide chase as you and the Acme Detective Agency pursue the infamous and elusive Carmen Sandiego and her gang as they rip-off the world's most famous landmarks and treasures.

The Deluxe Edition on CD-ROM includes: 3,200 clues about world geography, history and culture, *The World Almanac and Book of Facts* to help decipher clues (what a bonus!), the Official Acme dossier with photos and detailed background on all twenty gang members, images from the National Geographic Society, The Image Bank and Magnum photos, plus traditional and folk music from Smithsonian/Folkways Recordings, five levels of difficulty commensurate with your detective skills.

The CD-ROM version features eleven talking characters, hundreds of amusing animations, over 500 foreign-language clues, over 130 digitized images, and 150 authentic folk music recordings.

A movie-like musical score and realistic digitized sound makes it easy to forget that you're playing a game on your PC and really imparts the feeling that your really part of the action.

Twenty villains, Sixty countries, Sixteen maps, and 3,200 clues—what more could you ask for? The game is educational, entertaining, fun and can even be called addictive once you get into it. Hmmm, I wonder where Carmen and her gang is right about now....

CD-ROM REVIEW

Title: **Wild Places**
Format(s): **MPC, Mac and PC**
Publisher: **Aris Entertainment**
List Price: **$39.95**

Wild Places is one of the titles in Aris' *MediaClips* Series. The disc is a hybrid that works properly on Macintosh computers as well as DOS and MPC machines.

Wild Places takes you on an exploration of breathtaking vistas that you could only have imagined. You'll see nature as you have never looked at it before—the stunning photography unfolds before your eyes. Deserts, rocks, forests, and seascapes are part of the beauty and tranquillity of untamed North America.

Natural beauty is celebrated and presented with 100 excellent photographic images and fifty original audio clips and sound effects that can be reproduced royalty free.

In addition to *Wild Places*, the *MediaClips* series also includes *WorldView* (space), *Majestic Places* (mountains), *Money, Money, Money!* (cash), *Business Backgrounds* (assorted backgrounds), and *Full Bloom* (flora and fauna). Additionally, Aris has released two two-disc *MediaClips* titles: *Island Designs* is a collection of images of island fabrics including antique Hawaiian prints and authentic Balinese Batik prints (200 photos, 150 audio clips and sound effects); *Jets & Props* is a collection of the best images of civilian and military aircraft powered by—you guessed it—jets and props. This disc includes 200 photos, fifty movies of aircraft and 200 rock 'n roll and instrumental audio clips. All discs in the *MediaClips* series carry suggested retail prices of $39.95 to $59.95.

CD-ROM REVIEW

Title: Wing Commander II Deluxe Edition
Format(s): PC
Publisher: Origin Systems
List Price: $99.95

On this deluxe CD-ROM edition you get the whole Wing Commander accessory ensemble in addition to Origin's best selling action/flight simulation, *Wing Commander II.*

The game itself is composed of forty-seven harrowing missions that test your mettle and reflexes as you engage in dogfights, employ evasive maneuvers and make strategic decisions in split seconds. The *Special Operations* pack is also included on the CD-ROM which provides twenty additional missions that are even more difficult. If and when you have enough of the "right stuff" to succeed here, *Special Operations II* is also included on the disc to put twenty additional highly difficult missions on your duty roster.

The *Wing Commander II Speech Accessory Pack* is also included on the disc, and this endows the game with digitized speech (you can hear radio messages from your wingmen and foes), additional audio effects and significantly-enhanced realism.

A SoundBlaster or compatible sound card is required for digital speech playback, and an AdLib, SoundBlaster, Roland, or compatible audio card is required to enjoy the musical portions of the game. The musical score "senses" the action on-screen and alters the tempo and mood of the music to match—very dramatic!

With *Wing Commander II* you can step into the middle of all the action and drama you'd expect from a major motion picture, but now you're the star. You'll encounter enemies who match your skill level to make every battle a seat-squirmer. Go for it!

CD-ROM
REVIEW

Title: Word Tales
Format(s): Mac
Publisher: Warner New Media
List Price: $59.99

What a marvelous educational and entertaining CD-ROM for children aged 4 to 7 who have access to a Macintosh II-series or LC computer equipped with a CD-ROM drive.

Word Tales is simple to use. Children can play on their own or grown-ups can share in their discoveries. In fact, it's so clever, you may find yourself playing a *Word Tale* of your own.

The subject matter is colorful and geared to hold the child's interest for hours. *Word Tales* features colorful animated scenes that encourage exploration and learning. Youngsters can discover a jungle complete with jewels and jaguars or play volleyball with a visor-wearing vulture!

With the "What is the first letter of _lphabet?" game, kids get to fill in the missing letter to learn how letters combine to form words. They can select additional objects which begin with the same letter sound to learn how words represent objects.

Word Tales rewards the child with animated surprise endings. For example, complete a list of "K" words and you get to see the king and his kissing kitten live happily ever after.

The software requires a color monitor, at least 2.2 megabytes of free memory and System Software 6.0.7 or later.

Everything about this outstanding educational CD-ROM for very-youngsters is excellent: sound, graphics, animated sequences, and interface are all designed to hold the child's attention while providing an excellent head start for literacy.

CD-ROM REVIEW

Title: World Almanac and Book of Facts/1992
Format(s): MPC and Mac
Publisher: Metatec/Discovery Systems
List Price: $79.95

The 1992 CD-ROM edition of *The World Almanac and Book of Facts* is a compendium of contemporary information that appeals to a wide cross-section of users in Macintosh and PC formats (individual discs for each format).

The World Almanac has been a national best-seller and leading authority since 1868. The 1992 CD-ROM edition provides the user with even faster access to more than one million up-to-date facts and comprehensive coverage of the year's leading issues.

Highlights of this disc include the 1990 Census, Columbus' Discovery of America, Major Actions of Congress, Major Decisions of the Supreme Court (1990-1991), the Persian Gulf War, the 1991 World Series, coverage of the Soviet Union upheaval, and a section on the Scientific Achievements and Discoveries.

To make locating the particular information you want easier, extensive search capabilities are included in the software. The information is presented in menu format, with ten main menu choices: All Sections, Year In Review, Economics, 1990 Census, Noted Personalities, Sports, States of the Union, Nations of the World, Astronomy and Calendar, and Consumer Information.

The contents of the database can also be browsed, which is an entertaining and informative way of using the disc as well. This disc is an excellent information resource for home, business, educational or general reference applications and makes a worthwhile addition to any CD-ROM library.

Title: WorldView
Format(s): MPC, Mac, and PC
Publisher: Aris Entertainment
List Price: $49.95

Part of Aris' *MediaClips* series, *WorldView* is an absolutely breathtaking collection of 100 photos of the Earth, planets and solar system taken from the space shuttles and other spacecraft.

The disc provides both manual and automatic slide shows, complete with excellent "new age" musical accompaniments. Individual photos can also be viewed in small or large sizes, with or without captions, from the disc's GUI user interface.

Over 100 audio clips consisting of recordings of dialogue between Houston and astronauts in space, Neil Armstrong's historic words as the first man to set foot on the moon and more are included in addition to the musical selections.

Twenty-five movies are also included on the disc for users with MPC or Macintosh computers (sorry, these don't work from DOS on non-MPC machines), and they include the first lunar landing, shuttle takeoffs/landings, planet "flybys" and more.

It's a "heavenly" disc that's really "out of this world".

FIGURE 8.15 A stunning view of the Earth's western hemisphere as seen from Apollo 8. Clips, sounds and photos from WorldView can be copied royalty-free for non-commercial uses.

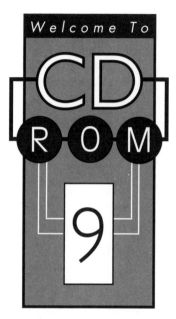

Welcome To

CD ROM

9

WHAT'S ON THE HORIZON?

In this lesson...

...CD-ROM's continuing evolution

...What we can look forward to in the near future

...CD-ROM as a personal publishing medium

...Rewritable optical media

...A few last terms and definitions

CD-ROM and optical data technology are in a state of flux, an ongoing evolution. Knowledge and technology both have a way of dynamically increasing their total sums so that more is known and accomplished in less time than ever before. CD-ROM is the classic example of a technology that enabled significant advances to be made while spawning additional technologies in the process.

In just a few short years we have watched a technological Genesis take place. From audio CDs came computer CD-ROMs; CD-ROM then spawned Philips CD-I, Kodak Photo CD, Sony MM/CD, CD/XA, and all of the other offshoot formats. Undoubtedly more evolutionary and proprietary formats will follow.

MM/CD is an informal designation used for Sony's portable Multimedia CD-ROM player, which, is a CD/XA format.

Within the next two to three years, or possibly sooner, there will be a "shakeout," and only those formats with the strongest and largest user bases will prevail. The less popular formats, just like Betamax videotape, will fall by the wayside.

ISO 9660 and the Macintosh HFS formats are here to stay, as is Redbook (standard CD) audio. Some of these ancillary formats will also gain mainstream acceptance as well. I predict Sony's CD/XA format, Philips CD-I, Tandy/Memorex VIS and Kodak's Photo CD will be the formats that are here for the long-term.

The next generation of CD-ROM drives, in addition to providing ever faster access times and better data transfer rates, will also have a high degree of format compatibility. These drives will, by benefit of sophisticated firmware, be able to read non-computer CD-ROM formats such as CD-I, for example. With the proper software loaded on the host PC you'll then be able to use the CD-I application on your computer.

Format compatibility will extend to the consumer machines as well, so that media designed for one type of home player can be used on another brand and type of machine. This will be accomplished primarily through firmware upgrades. We'll also see a proliferation of expansion accessories such as keyboards, expander cartridges, modems, disk drives, and printers for these machines coming in the relatively near future (many of these players already have expansion capabilities built into them). As the general public becomes more familiar with these players, their desire to do more and experience more with them will increase, making these expansion accessories a logical way to extend the device's appeal and usefulness.

As we're already seeing with machines like the Sony MDP-1100 MultiDisc Player, different optical formats will be playable on dedicated stand-alone devices. The Sony MDP-1100, for example, can play 12-inch and 8-inch laser discs, 5-inch audio CDs and CDV discs, as well as 3-inch audio CD "singles." Adding CD/XA, Photo CD and other format capabilities to machines such as this is not technologically difficult and is but another logical progression for the technology. As with all other mainstream products, consumer demand will dictate how fast the manufacturers respond in adding these additional capabilities as well as how much these machines will cost.

CDV is an acronym for Compact Disc Video, which is a compact disc format that can hold up to five minutes of full-motion video and up to twenty minutes of CD audio. CDV requires a special CDV player to access the video data.

Personal publishing workstations that are capable of creating one-off (CD/WO) discs will gain in popularity and prices will drop to the under-$5,000 mark (currently these machines are over $7,000). We'll see lots of personally-published CD-ROMs being used in the corporate world to hold proprietary client databases, parts catalogs, inventory references, actuarial tables, and more.

CD/WO is an abbreviation for Compact Disc/Write Once, also called a "one-off," since a single copy is made at a time. The media used is a special kind of compact disc that can be written-to using a special writable drive. One-offs are useful for creating test discs before sending data for mastering and replication. Since these discs conform to the ISO 9660 standard, they are playable in CD-ROM drives. One-offs are gold in color on the label side of the disc, and a dark green color on the data side.

High-volume users with applications that require archiving, storing and retrieving large amounts of information will find that personal publishing workstations can be invaluable for creating single-copy CD-ROMs. For example, libraries will find them attractive for creating CD-ROM card catalogs, for keeping periodicals and other documents available and accessible in a more permanent format than paper, and for many other such uses. City and state governments will find them attractive for creating CD-ROMs of the tax rolls, residents, voter registration, and myriad other uses.

Authors, too, will find personal CD-ROM publishing appealing, especially with works that could benefit from the rich multimedia environment that CD-ROM can provide. Authors who seek to put their works into distribution will find the one-offs produced by a personal publishing workstation to be ideal for submitting to the replicator for duplication.

While prices will get lower for these CD-writable workstations, they won't become an affordable peripheral for the average user who only needs an occasional one-off. To fill this need we will see "service agencies" cropping up that will provide personal publishing services to produce one-offs of computer CD-ROMs as well as other CD formats, including audio CDs and Kodak's Photo CD.

Magneto-Optical (MO) devices such as the IBM 3.5 inch Rewritable Drive and other brands which are already widely available will continue to grow in popularity as more people realize the benefits that removable, rewritable optical storage can provide. As this technology continues to evolve and improve we will see the advent of the affordable writable CD drive which utilizes an erasable medium that can be reused over and over again.

MO is an abbreviation for magneto-optical recording, which is a type of recording technology used with optical discs in which a laser beam heats a small portion of the magnetic material covering the disc. The heating enables a weak magnetic field to change the orientation of the portion, thus recording data on the disc. The same process can be used to erase the disc as well, making it rewritable.

Full-motion video with synchronized sound is the next major development area that is currently just getting started as of this writing. We'll see algorithms and applications improve continually to the point where animation and rolling video become standard features of almost every CD-ROM application. We can look forward to the biggest and most significant advances in this area under the MPC and CD/XA formats, since such tasks require fast access times and high data transfer rates to work correctly.

Personal computers themselves will continue to become more powerful, have more memory, calculate faster, and be capable of running multiple applications simultaneously that are far more complex than those available today. With advanced operating systems such as Microsoft's Windows NT (New Technology) already in beta testing, the capabilities of the personal computer will be significantly expanded to perform tasks and run software which is being written even as you read this now.

Tomorrow's world is just around the corner, and it promises to be full of wonder and excitement. Just as CD-ROM has helped to usher-in the Information Age, it will continue to be a major component of the new products, software and uses for it that are yet to come.

And now you are a part of it, too! Thanks for allowing me to be your guide and teacher.

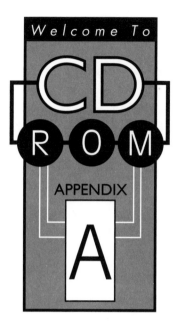

Welcome To
CD
ROM
APPENDIX
A

GLOSSARY

Access Time—The time required for a CD-ROM drive to respond to a request for data, measured in milliseconds (thousandths of a second). The access time spans the elapsed time from the point the information request was made until the information is received.

API—An abbreviation for Application Programming Interface, a set of routines than an application program uses to request and execute low-level services performed by the PC's operating system.

ASCII—(pronounced *ask-ee*) An acronym for the American Standard Code for Information Interchange. ASCII is an internationally-accepted coding scheme that assigns numeric values to letters, numbers, punctuation marks and control characters to enable computers to communicate with each other.

BMP—An abbreviation for bitmap, a data structure file format that describes a bit image by providing fixed coordinates for the x and y axes of each pixel comprising the image. Bitmaps are commonly used as the filetypes for images created with many drawing, paint, and graphics software programs.

Boolean operators—Also called logical operators, are conditional search parameters based upon Boolean algebra that check for logical conjunctions (AND), logical inclusions (OR), an exclusive or condition (XOR), and logical exclusions (NOT). Databases usually rely on Boolean operators to qualify the target data during searches.

Bridge disc—A disc that plays on a CD-XA drive or a CD-I drive. An XA disc stores a table of contents, permitting you to view the tracks when used with an audio drive. A CD-I does not—it changes at each sector and there is no table of contents. A bridge disc's low-level format allows it to be played on both XA or CD-I players. The Kodak Photo CD is an example of a bridge disc.

Buffer—A temporary holding area in memory where data is stored until an opportunity to complete its transfer arises. CD-ROM drives are equipped with built-in buffers that are used for data "streaming" or keeping a smooth and continuous flow of data coming at a constant rate of speed. The size of the buffer determines the sustained data transfer speed of the drive, with larger buffers (typically 64K to 128K) being preferable over smaller ones (16 or 32K).

Byte—A unit of information used in computer processing and storage consisting of 8 bits that, by their order, represent a single character.

Caddy—A thin plastic and metal magazine that is hinged on its top side to permit CD-ROMs to be inserted or removed from it. With a CD-ROM loaded in the caddy, the caddy is then inserted into the CD-ROM drive. Caddies provide a convenient means of loading and unloading CD-ROMs from the drive without touching the disc itself, and they also offer additional protection for the media.

CD-DA—An abbreviation for Compact Disc-Digital Audio. See Red Book for additional information on this standard.

CD-ROM—An acronym for Compact Disc Read-Only Memory. CD-ROM is an optical data storage medium for computers that uses laser light to read the binary information it contains.

CDV—An acronym for Compact Disc Video, CDV is a compact disc format that can hold up to five minutes of full-motion video and up to twenty minutes of CD audio. CDV requires a special CDV player to access the video data.

CD/WO—An abbreviation for Compact Disc/Write Once, also called a *one-off* since a single copy is made at a time. The media used is a special kind of compact disc that can be written to using a special writable drive. One-offs are useful for creating test discs before sending data for mastering and replication. Since these discs conform to the ISO 9660 standard, they are playable in CD-ROM drives. One-offs are gold in color on the label (non-data) side of the disc, and a dark green color on the data side.

CD/XA—Also frequently referred to as CD-ROM/XA. The XA designation stands for Extended Architecture, that uses both Mode 1 and Mode 2 (X/A). By mixing both modes on the same CD-ROM, low- to medium-fidelity digital audio can be simultaneously processed while data is viewed. The X/A standard was jointly developed and announced by Philips, Sony, and Microsoft in August 1988. CD-ROM/XA discs can be played on a standard CD-ROM drive, but a CD-ROM X/A controller card is required in the PC to access X/A capabilities.

Clip-Art—Any collection of proprietary or public domain photographs, diagrams, maps, drawings, or other such graphics that can be "clipped" from the collection and incorporated into other documents or applications.

CPU—An acronym for Central Processing Unit, a CPU is the "brain" of the computer that actually performs the computations and controls the operations of the machine. The CPU interprets and executes instructions that enable the computer to do useful work. In personal computers, the CPUs are also called *microprocessors* since they are contained entirely on a single chip. The microprocessor fetches, decodes, and executes instructions that enable the computer to do its work. The CPU also transfers information to and from other resources (such as RAM and disk drives) that comprise the host computer system.

Daisychaining—A term that describes two or more devices linked together through each other to the same PC. The first device is connected directly to the PC, while the second device is connected to the first. The third device is connected to the second, fourth to third, and so forth. Signals are passed through the "chain" back-and-forth from the computer to the desired device, and to avoid confusion or conflicts, each device in the chain is given its own unique ID.

Database—Any aggregate collection of data. Relating to computers and CD-ROM, a database is a file or files composed of individual records for each entry in a file. Each record is composed of separate fields that can be used for searching, sorting, or separating specific information.

Digital—Relating to digits or the way they are represented. For all practical purposes here, digital is synonymous with binary because personal computers store and process information coded as combinations of binary digits (bits).

DIN Connector—A round, multi-pin connector that conforms to the German national standards organization specification (Deutsch Industrie Norm). DIN connectors usually connect the keyboard to the PC's main system unit, and the most frequent configurations are either 5-pin or 8-pin connectors.

DOS-Based—Any application or utility that operates directly from the MS-DOS operating system rather than through an alternate environment or operating system, such as Windows or OS/2.

EISA—An acronym for Extended Industry Standard Architecture, a bus standard introduced in 1988. EISA maintains backward compatibility with ISA (Industry Standard Architecture) in addition to adding many of the enhanced features IBM introduced with its Micro Channel Architecture bus standard including a 32-bit data path.

EPS—An abbreviation for Encapsulated PostScript. A set of PostScript commands that can be used as an independent entity for data such as clip-art.

Firmware—Software instructions, such as start-up routines, low-level input/output instructions, and so forth that are stored in read-only memory (ROM). Unlike RAM (Random Access Memory), which "forgets" all that is contained in it when power is removed, ROM "remembers" all that is programmed into it, making it ideal for instructions and information that is needed by the device on a permanent basis.

Front End—A term that is sometimes used to describe the user interface of a software product. It can also refer to the primary stage of a multi-stage hardware device.

Gigabyte—(pronounced either *jig-a-bite* or *gig-a-bite*) A term that represents 1 billion bytes (1,048,567x1,024 = 1,073,741,824 bytes). Abbreviated GB, it is used to express truly huge capacities of several hundred megabytes (for example, .5GB).

GUI—(pronounced *goo-ee*) An acronym for Graphical User Interface. GUIs use icons, drop-down menus, and other visual representations to initiate computer commands, run programs, exchange files, and perform other tasks using a mouse and/or keyboard, rather than typed commands. GUIs are more intuitive and easier to use than entering commands directly at the system command prompt. The Apple Macintosh, Microsoft Windows, and IBM's OS/2 are all examples of GUIs.

Hardware-dependent/Hardware-independent—Specifically designed and intended for use with a particular hardware device or operating environment. A proprietary-interfaced CD-ROM drive is hardware-dependent because it only works with a proprietary interface designed specifically for it and a specific type of computer system. Conversely, a SCSI-interfaced CD-ROM drive is hardware-independent since it works with any computer system equipped with a SCSI port.

HFS—An abbreviation for Hierarchical File System, a tree-structured file system on the Apple Macintosh in which folders can be "nested" within other folders. Early versions of the Macintosh operating systems (known as MFS, for Macintosh File System) supported only a flat file system with no folders or subdirectories.

High Sierra—An industry-wide drafted format specification for CD-ROM that defines the logical structure, file structure, and record structures of a CD-ROM disc. It served as the basis for ISO-9660, the formal international format standard for CD-ROM. High Sierra was named for the location of a meeting for CD-ROM industry representatives held near Lake Tahoe in November, 1985 where the standard was drafted.

Host PC—The main personal computer (in a single-user, non-networked system) that controls and utilizes all other connected devices including drives, printers, monitor, keyboard, mouse, joystick, and more. Since the PC provides the logic, input-output, memory storage, computing, and in many cases the actual operational voltage, the PC *hosts* all of the devices as if they were *guests*.

Hybrid Disc—A CD-ROM that contains data written in two formats, HFS and ISO 9660, thus enabling the disc to be read and used by a Macintosh or an IBM-compatible PC. The data is written in two discrete locations on the disc.

Hypercard—Software designed for the Apple Macintosh that provides users with an information management tool that uses a series of "cards" collected in a "stack." Each card represents a record for an individual item or data category and can contain text, graphical images, and sound.

Hypertext—A means of linking and presenting information using target words within the text as the "hot links" that trigger hypertext jumps. Using hypertext, related information (which may be textual, pictorial, audio or video in nature) can be accessed in a totally non-sequential way, permitting the user to jump about and explore topics of interest entirely at will.

Information Age—A term used in Alvin Toffler's book *The Third Wave*, that refers to the phase of societal development we have recently entered due to microprocessor-controlled electronic devices. The Information Age was ushered-in by the advent of satellites, personal computers, fax machines, cellular phones, and increased communication efficiency. The ability to gather, correlate, sort, exchange, and deploy information instantaneously is the "product" and most important commodity of the Information Age. Data and data-related services will replace agriculture and manufacturing as the mainstay industries of the economy in the Information Age.

Interface—The point at which two elements in a computer system connect and communicate. Different types of interfaces are present at different levels of computing, ranging from the user interface that enables the user to interact with the computer to the hardware interface that makes connecting external devices to the PC possible.

ISA—An acronym for Industry Standard Architec-ture, the widely accepted (but unofficial) designation for the bus design of the original IBM PC. The ISA specification was expanded to include a 16-bit data path in 1984 from its original 8-bit specification with the introduction of the IBM PC/AT computer.

ISO 9660—An international standard format for CD-ROM adopted by the International Organization for Standardization. This is the "legal" name for the High Sierra draft standard of the specification, with some modifications and enhancements.

Jewel box—A thin, almost-square hinged plastic case in which CD-ROMs and audio CDs come packed. In addition to protecting the disc during shipment, the jewel box also provides a place to store the disc when it is not in use in the drive or in a caddy, thus protecting it from dirt, scratches, and other foreign matter that could damage it or impair its readability.

Kilobyte—(abbreviated KB, K, or Kbyte) The equivalent of 1,024 bytes. Kilobytes are usually used to express capacities of RAM, floppy diskettes, files, and other measures less than a megabyte (1024x1024=1,048,576 bytes) in size.

LCD—An abbreviation for Liquid Crystal Display, a type of display that uses a liquid compound having a structure that makes different character patterns visible when electrical voltage is applied to it. Many wristwatches and portable consumer electronics devices use LCD displays.

Magneto-optical—See entry under MO.

MCA—An acronym for Micro Channel Architecture, the design of the bus used in IBM PS/2 computers (except for the Model 25 and Model 30). Micro Channel expansion slots are electrically and physically different from the standard IBM PC/AT (ISA) bus, so accessory or adapter cards for standard IBM-compatible PC's don't work in a Micro Channel machine.

Megabyte—(abbreviated MB) The measurement term used to represent 1,048,576 bytes (1024x1024 bytes). Megabytes are used to express large capacities when referring to total system RAM memory, large disk drives, and CD-ROM data capacities.

Megahertz—(abbreviated MHz) A measure of electronic frequency equivalent to 1,000,000 cycles-per-second. The computational speed of a personal computer is dependent on the type and speed of its CPU, as measured in megahertz. A PC with a 12MHz CPU is oscillating at twice the speed of the same PC with a 6MHz microprocessor of the same type.

Magnetic Media—A term referring to floppy diskettes, hard disks, tape backup units, or other devices that use magnetism (rather than light and optics) to write and read data.

Microfiche—A non-computerized storage medium that uses a sheet of photographic film to record highly-reduced images of entire pages of data too small to be read with the naked eye. A projection machine, called a microfiche reader, enlarges the microfiche images for reading or reference.

MM/CD—An informal designation used for Sony's portable MultiMedia CD-ROM player that, in reality, is CD/XA format variety.

MO—An abbreviation for magneto-optical recording, a type of recording technology used with optical discs in which a laser beam heats a small portion of the magnetic material covering the disc. The heating enables a weak magnetic field to change the orientation of the portion, thus recording data on the disc. The same process can be used to erase the disc as well, making it rewritable.

Mode 1—An encoding scheme used in producing CD-ROM that utilizes three (3) layers of error detection and correction for maintaining the integrity of computer data.

Mode 2—An encoding scheme used in producing CD-ROM that provides two (2) layers of error detection and correction, used most often with audio or compressed audio/video data (such as sound and full-motion video).

Motherboard—The main circuit board containing the primary "system critical" components for a microcomputer system. The components that are found on the motherboard include the CPU, main memory and controller circuitry required for the expansion bus and expansion slots in addition to other components required for the proper operation of these circuits.

MSCDEX—An acronym for Microsoft CD Extensions, the system-level driver software from Microsoft that extends the normal capabilities of the MS-DOS operating system to utilize CD-ROM. As of this writing the current version of MSCDEX is 2.21. The MSCDEX.EXE file is normally included as a line in the AUTOEXEC.BAT file and loaded automatically when the PC is booted.

MS-DOS—(pronounced *em-ess-doss*) An acronym for Microsoft Disk Operating System. MS-DOS oversees and supervises the basic tasks and services required to run a computer including disk input and output, video support, keyboard control, and other essential functions.

Multi-session—A term that pertains to the Kodak Photo CD format. Multi-session Photo CDs contain images that were transferred during several different sessions, with each subsequent session generating its own table of contents for that session. The ability of CD-ROM drives and other consumer-level devices to read these discs varies from product to product. A drive (or device) is multi-session capable if it can read and display the images contained in all directories in the table of contents of a multi-session Photo CD. (See *single-session.*)

OEM—An acronym for Original Equipment Manufac-turer, this term often describes hardware or software versions that are provided on a wholesale basis to other manufacturers who include the device or program in their final, finished product (such as a computer system).

One-off—See entry under CD/WO.

Optical media—A term referring to CD-ROM or any other medium (such as a laserdisc) that utilizes light, lenses, mirrors, or other optical components for the storage and retrieval of data.

PCX—A very popular bitmap file type developed by Z-Soft that is used for storing scanned photos, graphics, and images created with numerous draw, paint, and scanning applications software packages.

PIC/PICT—A common bitmap file type frequently used for storing image files such as scanned photos, graphics, and clip-art images.

Pigtail connector—An electrical power connector consisting of a set of four colored wires (one yellow, two black, one red) originating at the PC's power supply that has a socketed white nylon connector at its end. The sockets on this connector mate with contact pins on an internally-

mounted drive device (CD-ROM drive, floppy drive, hard drive, or tape backup drive). The nylon connector is "keyed" with slanted corners on two sides that prevents it from being inserted incorrectly.

Public domain software—Any program donated for public use by its owner or developer and freely available for copying and distribution.

QuickTime—Apple Computer's proprietary means of playing compressed full-motion video images with synchronized sound. QuickTime is an extension to the Apple System Software.

RAM—An acronym for Random Access Memory. RAM refers to semiconductor-based (silicon chip-based) memory that can be read and written by the microprocessor or other devices in the computer system. RAM is classified as *volatile* (rather than *stable*) memory, since it loses all of its stored data when power is interrupted or removed (the computer is shut off).

Red Book—The standard specification for CD Audio as detailed and agreed upon by Philips, Sony, and other major manufacturers. Since these technical specifications were published in a book with a red cover, this specification for audio became known as the Red Book standard.

Shareware—Copyrighted software that is distributed free of charge but is usually accompanied by a request for a small payment from satisfied users to cover costs and registration for documentation and program updates.

SCSI—(pronounced *scuzzy*) An acronym that stands for Small Computer System Interface. SCSI is a standard high-speed parallel interface as defined by the X3T9.2 committee of the American National Standards Institute that permits devices such as CD-ROM drives, hard disks, and printers to be connected to microcomputers.

SCSI-2—An evolved SCSI standard as drafted by the American National Standards Institute that seeks to alleviate some of the compatibility problems sometimes encountered using SCSI devices by providing more stringent hardware design guidelines, additional device commands, bettor error handling and recovery, and enhanced logic for signal routing and device sharing. It is important to note that not all SCSI adapter cards can support newer devices that are built to conform to the SCSI-2 protocols.

Single-session—A term pertaining to the Kodak Photo CD. Single-session Photo CDs are discs that have had all of their images transferred onto them in one single session, and one table of contents for the disc is generated. A drive is said to be single-session capable if it can display the images listed on the disc's single table of contents. A single session drive only displays the images of the original table of contents if a multi-session Photo CD is being used. (See *multi-session.*)

SVGA—An acronym for Super VGA, a superset of the original VGA specification that yields higher resolution. 640x480/256-color, 800x600, and 1024x768 resolutions are all considered to be SVGA operational modes and are gaining popularity rapidly. SVGA is preferred for any intensely graphic applications and is particularly well-suited for CD-ROM.

TIF/TIFF—Abbreviations for Tagged Image File Format, a standard bitmap file format commonly used for scanning, storage, and interchange of grayscale images.

Transparent device—A device that performs its own tasks, usually while sharing a resource such as a system port, without affecting or impeding the operation of any other component in the system. During use, a transparent device is said to be "invisible" to the user since the usage is occurring without the user's knowledge.

TSR—An abbreviation for Terminate and Stay Resident, which denotes a type of program running under MS-DOS that remains loaded in memory even when it is not running so that it can be quickly invoked for a specific task while in another application.

VGA—An acronym for Video Graphics Array, a video adapter introduced in 1987 by IBM. VGA provides moderately high resolution screen images up to a maximum of 640 horizontal pixels by 480 vertical pixels in either 2 or 16 colors from a 262,144-color palette. VGA's low-resolution mode provides screen-image resolution of 320 horizontal pixels by 200 vertical pixels with 256 colors simultaneously displayable from the same 262,144-color palette. VGA is the minimum video standard that should be considered for CD-ROM applications, with SVGA being preferable. (See *SVGA.*)

Windows—The popular name for Microsoft Windows, a multitasking graphical user interface environment that runs on MS-DOS-based computers. Drop-down menus, screen windows, and icons that represent entire programs or specific tasks are all features of Windows that make most computer tasks simply a matter of pointing with a mouse and clicking one of the mouse buttons to activate that application or utility.

Windows NT—Microsoft's graphical-based operating system that provides true pre-emptive multi-tasking and 32-bit data paths. The NT designation stands for New Technology.

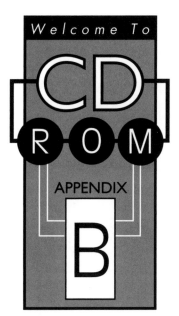

Welcome To
CD ROM
APPENDIX
B

HOW CD-ROMS ARE MADE

In preparing this book I visited Nimbus Information Systems in Ruckersville, VA, for a first-hand look at CD manufacturing. The parent company of the Information Systems Division is Nimbus Manufacturing, Inc., a U.S.-based company. Nimbus was formerly owned by Nimbus Records Ltd., based in the United Kingdom, a world-class producer of classical audio CD's for several years. Nimbus is a former recipient of the United Kingdom's prestigious Queen's Award for Technological Achievement, due in large part to the company's development of the Nimbus-Halliday laser mastering system. Nimbus started its information systems division in 1988 for the then-infant CD-ROM industry and has quickly moved to the forefront as a total-source publishing house.

Before the CD-ROM discs can be manufactured, the data they will contain must be put in a usable form, and this process is called pre-mastering. Nimbus is typical of most CD-ROM publishing and manufacturing facilities in that it can accept data in numerous formats from clients who wish to publish CD-ROM discs. These formats include files contained on floppy or hard drives, 9-track tape and other magnetic tape formats as well as hard-copy text and image data that can be scanned and captured. *One-off* discs, which are single-copy CD-ROMs made with a specialized CD drive that can write to special blank writable discs, can also be used as the data source. (Nimbus can produce one-offs for clients as well.)

Since CD-ROM has multimedia capabilities, audio and video information in numerous formats can also be included on the CD-ROM. The data is transferred from client-supplied media to huge multi-platter disk drives at a CD Publisher workstation console where it is arranged and consolidated on the magnetic media. Appropriate indexing, sync, and error detection and correction information is added to the data, along with retrieval software and any other appropriate utility and setup files required by the application. In effect, these multi-disc platters produce a magnetic "working copy" of what the CD-ROM will be when it is finished. Lots of testing and checking takes place on this working copy to make sure the data has copied over from the client's media accurately and that everything is working as it should. If desired at this point, a one-off copy can be made that is readable by any standard CD-ROM drive which enables clients to "test drive" their software on optical media before replicating.

When everything checks out satisfactorily at the CD publishing station, the data on the magnetic working copy is transferred at the CD mastering station via the Nimbus-Halliday laser. This laser etches *pits* onto a perfectly flat and true glass master disc that has been uniformly coated with a photosensitive solution. This etched glass master is the matrix from which all duplicating is performed.

Inside the manufacturing facility are several areas that take care of various operations during the process. The first stop is the mastering area that is housed in a "class 1,000 clean room." The name denotes that there are less than 1,000 under-1/2-micron particles detectable in one cubic foot of air over a 15-minute period. This is several times cleaner than a hospital operating room and necessary for successful mastering up to Nimbus' standards since one particle of cigarette smoke can obscure up to fifty pits on a disc. I had to don a "clean suit" in a changing room before entering the mastering area.

The glass laser-etched matrix disc is then placed in an electroplating vat inside the clean room where a slow, steady current is passed through solution to layer the glass matrix with nickel coating. This plating process takes about four hours to produce the finest, most uniform crystal structure possible in the nickel. This nickel membrane, called the *mother*, bears the exact pit and land geography as the glass master, but in reverse relief. The original glass matrix is then stored safely in Nimbus' high-security vault and additional nickel mold masters (called *fathers*) are made by adding another layer of nickel to the mother in the plating tank and then separating the two halves.

In a setup area the father molds are readied for the casting machines and the centering holes are cut. Each father is good for up to 75,000 presses, so multiple fathers are prepped for large production runs.

The father is mounted in an injection molding machine where virgin polycarbonate pellets are heated to a gooey consistency and then injected under 62 tons of pressure against the nickel father. The mold is then rapidly cooled to solidify the plastic and the injection spline is snapped off, leaving a perfectly concentric hole in the hub of the transparent plastic disc. A robotic arm then moves the disc to the metalizing machine while the injection molder closes and more molten polycarbonate is pumped in under pressure to create the next disc. The entire operation takes only 4.5 seconds and Nimbus has fourteen injection presses in operation at present with plans to add more in the near future. The company's present production capability is better than 150,000 CD-ROM discs per day.

The metalizing process takes the newly-molded polycarbonate disc into a chamber where it is exposed to vaporized aluminum oxide which coats the pitted side of the disc with a uniform 1-micron layer of aluminum to provide reflectivity for the laser light. This metalizing operation takes only a few seconds as well.

To prevent oxidation and contamination of the disc's new aluminum surface, a coating of optically transparent lacquer is applied to form an air-tight seal over the thin layer of metal. To accomplish this, the newly metalized discs are conveyed to a lacquer application station where a thick bead of lacquer is applied in a concentric ring close to the disc's hub. It is then transferred to a spinning drum a few inches away where the disc goes from 0 to 10,000 RPM in less than a second. The lacquer is evenly dispersed due to centrifugal force and the disc is then moved to a drying station which has an ultraviolet (UV) light to cure the lacquer in seconds.

Quality assurance is an integral part of the manufacturing process and interim QA checks take place at virtually every step of the way. Nimbus personnel check the discs for stress marks under polarized lenses to ensure optimal concentricity, flatness, and freedom from defects. Automated block error checking is performed on one of every fifty discs produced to confirm manufacturing integrity, and every disc is tested at 24 million points for a variety of faults.

Label data is imprinted on the plastic (non-metalized) side of the disc using a soft-rubber stamper to produce an image transfer (like silk-screening) that is impactless. Up to two colors are considered standard for labeling, although Nimbus imprints three or more colors if the client so desires it. Label imprinting is cured under UV light and the finished discs are moved to the final inspection area for additional QA checking before packaging.

Nimbus also provides imprinting of the front and back liners for the jewel boxes as well as shrink-wrapping services.

The cost of publishing a CD-ROM is surprisingly inexpensive when you consider the massive amount of information you can include on a single disc. Using Nimbus as an example, you can publish several hundred megabytes of data on a CD-ROM for under $2,000 complete. That includes pre-mastering, mastering, molding, imprinting, assembling, and shrink-wrapping 200 CD-ROM discs.

Without a doubt, CD-ROM is the most inexpensive publishing medium possible on a cost-per-character basis.

If you'd like additional information on Nimbus' CD-ROM publishing services, contact:

Larry Boden, National Sales Manager
Nimbus Information Systems, Inc.
P.O. Box 7305
Charlottesville, VA 22906
(804) 985-1100 / Fax (804) 985-4625

The following pictures, photographed by Liz Benford, illustrate some of the major steps in the CD-ROM manufacturing process.

FIGURE B.1 *Data is transferred from client-supplied media to huge multi-platter disk drives at one of the CD Publisher workstation consoles, shown above. Indexing, sync, and error correction information are added to the data, along with retrieval software and any other appropriate utility/setup files required by the application. In effect, these multi-disc platters produce a magnetic "working copy" of what the CD-ROM will be like when it is finished.*

FIGURE B.2 *The robotic arm shown above is transporting a newly-molded compact disc from the injection molding machine to the metalizing machine where it is exposed to vaporized aluminum oxide that coats the pitted side of the disc with a uniform 1-micron layer of aluminum to provide reflectivity for the laser light. Injection molding and flash-cooling the disc takes about 4.5 seconds, and the metalizing process takes only a few seconds as well.*

FIGURE B.3 *Quality assurance testing is performed several times during the manufacturing process. At the QA station shown above the discs are checked for stress marks under polarized lenses to ensure optimal concentricity, flatness, and freedom from defects.*

FIGURE B.4 *The Nimbus production facilities are highly automated, as shown above, with this automated conveyor system that eliminates physical handling to a large degree. This newly-metalized disc is on its way to the lacquering station.*

FIGURE B.5 *A concentric bead of optically-transparent lacquer is applied to the discs near the hub and they are spun at very high speed to disperse the lacquer evenly over the discs' surface. The lacquer provides an airtight seal for the metalized surface of the disc to protect it from oxidation, airborne particles, fingerprints, and other contaminants that could jeopardize the integrity of the data. The lacquer is "quick cured" using UV lights.*

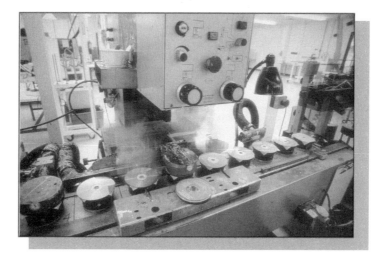

FIGURE B.6 *The discs next move to the imprinting station where an impactless stamp applies the label printing. The process is similar to silk-screening, and Nimbus can provide multi-color imprinting to give clients' CDs a unique appearance.*

FIGURE B.7 *More QA testing is performed before the discs are given a final okay. In addition to human testers, as shown above, computer-automated testing is also performed that checks the discs at several million individual points to ensure they are free of defects.*

FIGURE B.8 *The packaging station is the last stop for the compact discs. In the photo above the discs are being inserted into their jewel cases, which already have their printed front and back liners inserted. Once the discs are inserted the jewel cases are closed and can be shrink-wrapped if desired. Since the manufacturing process is virtually identical for CD audio, CD-ROM, CD-I, or any other compact disc format, Nimbus can and does make all of these formats for its clients.*

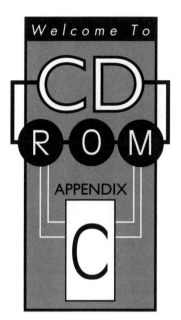

Welcome To

CD ROM

APPENDIX

C

How CD-ROMs and Drives Work

CD-ROM is based on the same optical and digital storage technology used by audio compact discs. Data is encoded and stored on a subsurface within a clear polycarbonate disc, and the subsurface is metalized with a thin coating to provide reflectivity. The data (which can be text, audio, video or a combination of all three) is stored on a single continuous spiraling track that starts at the center (hub) of the disc and continues outward toward the edges. Each successive turn of the spiral is just under 1.6 microns from the next one, yielding slightly more than 16,000 tracks per inch (a considerably more efficient arrangement than the 96 tracks per inch found on high-density 5.25-inch magnetic floppy disks). The track itself is composed of billions of microscopic indentations called *pits* that are separated from each other by flat areas called *lands*.

A gallium arsenide laser beam housed within the optical reading head of the CD-ROM drive passes through a special collimating lens that makes light rays travel in parallel. An objective lens converges these parallel light rays into a single point that is focused on the spinning compact disc.

The speed of the disc varies with the position of the laser beam on the disc's radius. The disc rotates faster when reading the inner tracks than it does reading the outer tracks so that the rate of data streaming stays the same. Thus, CD-ROM is classified as a CLV (constant linear velocity) device.

The pits on the disc surface scatter the light so that only a small portion is reflected back to the optical read head. Conversely, the lands reflect a significantly greater amount of light to the read head. A photo detector reads the intensity of the reflected light and converts it into current, giving a low current assignment to the proportionately low reflectivity of the pits and assigning it a "1" value. The higher reflectivity of the lands results in a "0" value assignment because of the increased current flow generated, and this is what produces the binary digital code which can be utilized by your computer. This binary code is read by the drive at the rate of seventy-five 2,048-byte sectors (or 150K-bytes) per second.

It goes without saying that the arrangement and spacing of the pits and lands must be quite exact, and due to their microscopic size, dust and other foreign particles can really wreak havoc in the overall scheme of things here. Error correction, therefore, is absolutely essential. Dual error correction techniques are used to provide a fail-safe mechanism of retrieving and/or restoring data. The first technique involves mixing a redundant level of data with the original data, and scrambling it within a block so that logically-contiguous data is not *physically* contiguous. The second technique involves error-correction algorithms performed by the host computer from information provided on the ECC (error correction coding) tracks of the disc itself. The end result is a remarkably reliable system for retrieving data from the compact disc which has a reconstructive rate failure of only 1 bit in every *quadrillion*.

Two predominant data encoding standards prevail for CD-ROM: the Macintosh HFS (Hierarchical File System), a tree-structured file system on the Apple Macintosh in which folders can be "nested" within other folders, and the ISO 9660 data format standard. The ISO 9660 standard is based on the original High Sierra standard draft, with the addition of some additional enhancements to the specification. For all practical purposes, virtually every computer CD-ROM drive sold today can read both the HFS and ISO-9660 formats without any problem, provided the Microsoft disc extensions version 2.0 or newer (2.21 is the most current version number as of this writing) or appropriate Macintosh file import extensions are used on the host computer. In short, unless you have a very old CD-ROM drive you shouldn't have any problem reading CD-ROM discs formatted to either one of these standards.

These images, along with their attendant captions, will aid you in understanding the technological miracle we call CD-ROM by illustrating the actual construction elements of the disc and how the laser beam and related optical components in a CD-ROM drive read the data and convert it from reflected light values into binary code which can be used and processed by the personal computer.

The source of the following figures are taken from Discovery Systems' *CD-ROM Sampler* disc, and they are used here with permission from Discovery Systems.

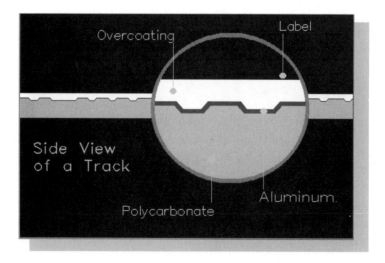

FIGURE C.1 *This cross-section view of a CD-ROM shows it various layers of construction. The disc is made of polycarbonate plastic, thinly coated with aluminum to provide reflectivity for laser light. The protective lacquer overcoating keeps the aluminized surface from oxidizing and becoming contaminated with fingerprints, airborne particles and other foreign material which could jeopardize the data.*

FIGURE C.2 *Unlike magnetic computer disks that store data on concentric data tracks, CD-ROM data streams in a continuous spiral track that starts at the center of the disc and works its way outward. The adjacent layers of data along the spiral path are less the 1.6 microns apart.*

FIGURE C.3 *Data tracks are composed of pits and lands, each of which produces a different reflectivity level for laser light. The reflected laser light is "read" by a photodetector to produce 1 and 0 binary patterns. Huge data storage capacity is the result of the less-than 1.6-micron track width, which yields an incredibly dense 16,000 tracks per inch (compared to a 96-track-per-inch floppy disk).*

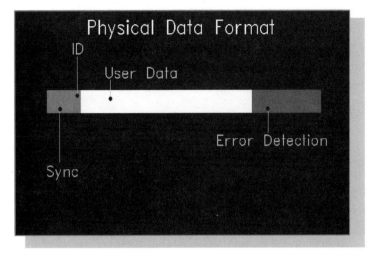

FIGURE C.4 *Data tracks on a CD-ROM are arranged in 2KB(2,048-byte) sectors for user data. Each block has an additional space allocated for sync, ID, user data, and error-detection. The sync and ID indexing uses time marks to facilitate fast access to any section of the disc despite its spiral track format.*

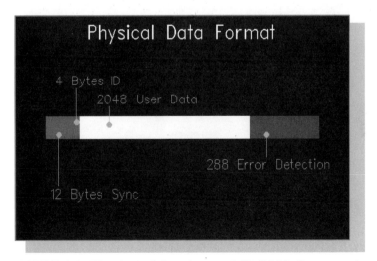

FIGURE C.5 *The physical data format of CD-ROM allocates twelve bytes for sync, 4 bytes for ID, and 288 bytes for error detection for each 2KB data sector. This accounts for extraordinary accuracy resulting in less than 1 error per quadrillion reads.*

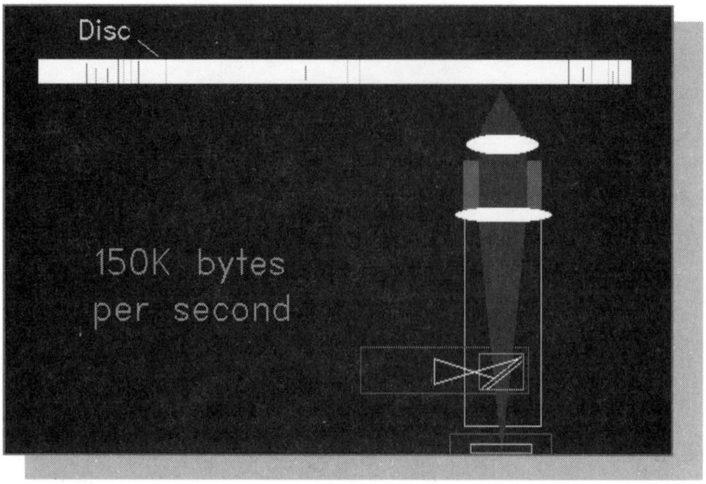

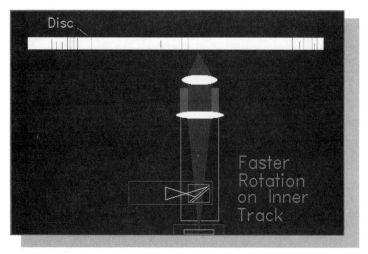

FIGURE C.6 *While initial seek time may be about 350 milliseconds, data transfers at a respectable rate of 150KB (seventy-five 2KB blocks) per second once the appropriate sector on the CD-ROM has been located.*

FIGURE C.7 *CD-ROM is a CLV (constant linear velocity) device, which means that its rotational speed varies with the position of the laser on the disc's radius.*

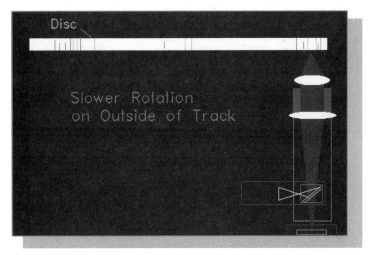

FIGURE C.8 *The CD-ROM disc rotates faster when the laser is reading data from the inner tracks than when it is reading outer tracks, since the track radius is smaller near the center than toward the edges of the disc.*

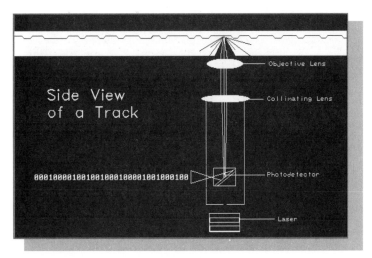

FIGURE C.9 *A gallium-arsenide laser beam passes through a collimating lens and is focused through an objective lens on the top surface of the spinning disc to read its pits and lands. The reflected light is interpreted by a photo detector, which assigns values of 1 and 0 to it, thus enabling the PC to work with the data.*

FIGURE C.10 *The CD-ROM drive searches the disc for subcode information as the read head moves across the disc. As the head nears its target the search is narrowed and direct block addresses are read.*

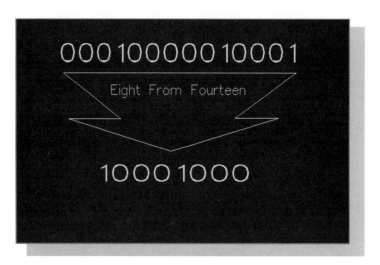

FIGURE C.11 *As bits are read from a disc, they are grouped to form 14-bit "words" for interpretation. Each 14-bit word is then reduced to an 8-bit word through a process known as EFM, which stands for Eight from Fourteen Modulation.*

FIGURE C.12 *Error detection and correction are extremely important in the overall picture of CD-ROM data storage and transfer. Extensive measures are implemented to ensure that data integrity is maintained despite physical damage to the disc. Two distinct methods of error detection and correction are used on CD-ROM discs.*

FIGURE C.13 *The Cross Interleaved Reed-Solomon Code, or CIRC method, is implemented in the hardware of the CD-ROM drive.*

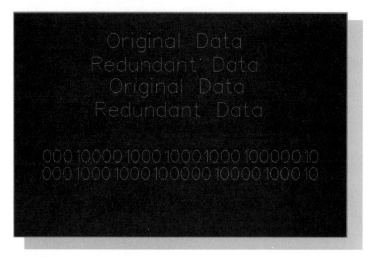

FIGURE C.14 *The CIRC method involves mixing a redundant level of data with the original data. The data is then scrambled so that the data within any given block on the disc that is logically contiguous is not physically contiguous. This ensures that data can be recovered if a read error is encountered.*

FIGURE C.15 *If an error cannot be corrected using CIRC, then the layered ECC is invoked. This is similar to CIRC, but is a more complex scheme where the error correction is performed by the host PC rather than by the CD-ROM drive itself. Redundant data levels are read and reassembled into their correct order to override the bad sectors and present the data as it was originally written.*

Manufacturers, Suppliers, and Software Publishers

CD-ROM Drive Manufacturers and Suppliers

Apple Computer, Inc.
20525 Mariani Avenue
Cupertino, CA 95014
(408) 996-1010

Always Technology Corporation
31336 Via Colinas, Suite 101
Westlake Village, CA 91362
(818) 597-1400

CD Technology, Inc.
766 San Aleso Avenue
Sunnyvale, CA 94086
(408) 752-8500

Chinon America Inc.
615 Hawaii Avenue
Torrance, CA 90503
(310) 533-0274

Denon Digital Industries
1380 Monticello Road
Madison, GA 30650
(404) 342-3425

Eastman Kodak Company
343 State Street
Rochester, NY 14650
(716) 724-4000

Hitachi Home Electronics (America), Inc.
401 West Artesla Boulevard
Compton, CA 90220
(310) 537-8383

IBM Corporation
1133 Westchester Avenue
White Plains, NY 10604
(800) 426-2468

NEC Technologies, Inc.
1255 Michael Drive
Wood Dale, IL 60191
(708) 860-9500

Panasonic Communications & Systems Company
Office Automation Division
Two Panasonic Way
Secaucus, NJ 07094
(201) 348-5200

Philips Interactive Media of America (CDI)
11111 Santa Monica Boulevard, Suite 750
Los Angeles, CA 90025
(310) 444-6619

Philips Consumer Electronics Company
One Philips Drive
P.O. Box 14810
Knoxville, TN 37914-1810
(800) 835-3506

Pioneer Communications of America, Inc.
600 East Crescent Avenue
Upper Saddle River, NJ 07458
(201) 327-6400

Procom Technology, Inc.
2181 Dupont
Irvine, CA 92715
(714) 549-9449

Sony Computer Peripheral Products Company
655 River Oaks Parkway
San Jose, CA 95134
(800) 352-7669

Tandy Corporation
1500 One Tandy Center
Fort Worth, TX 76102
(817) 390-3011

Trantor Systems, Ltd.
5415 Randall Place
Fremont, CA 94538
(510) 770-1400

CD-ROM SOFTWARE PUBLISHERS
(WITH TITLES REVIEWED IN LESSON 8)

Alde Publishing
6520 Edenvale Boulevard., Suite 118
Eden Prairie, MN 55346
(612) 934-4239

Aris Entertainment
444 Via Marina, Suite 811
Marina Del Rey, CA 90292
(310) 821-0234

Broderbund Software, Inc.
500 Redwood Boulevard—P.O. Box 6121
Novato, CA 94948
(415) 382-4568

Bureau Development, Inc.
141 New Road
Parsippany, NJ 07054
(201) 808-2700

Compton's New Media
2320 Camino Vida Roble
Carlsbad, CA 92009
(619) 929-2500

Corel Systems Corporation
1600 Carling Avenue
Ottawa, ON, Canada K1Z 8R7
(613) 728-8200

Cragsmoor Interactive
390 Riverside Drive, Suite 11D
New York, NY 10025
(212) 864-7547

Creative Multimedia Corporation
514 NW 11th Avenue, Suite 203
Portland, OR 97209
(503) 241-4351

Digital Gallery Limited
4440 SW Corbett, Suite 202
Portland, OR 97201
(800) 828-6369

EBook, Inc.
39315 The Zacate Avenue
Fremont, CA 94538
(510) 429-1331

EDUCORP
7434 Trade Street
San Diego, CA 92126
(619) 536-9999

G&G Designs/Communications
6359 Paseo Del Lago
Carlsbad, CA 92009
(619) 431-7400

Gazelle Technologies, Inc.
7434 Trade Street
San Diego, CA 92126
(619) 536-9999

Grolier Electronic Publishing, Inc.
Sherman Turnpike
Danbury, CT 06816
(800) 356-5590

HammerHead Publishing
220 South Military Trail
Deerfield Beach, FL 33442
(305) 426-8114

Information U.S.A., Inc.
P.O. Box E
Kensington, MD 20895
(800) 955-POWER

Macmillan New Media
124 Mt. Auburn Street
Cambridge, MA 02138
(617) 661-2955

Meckler Corporation
11 Ferry Lane West
Westport, CT 06880
(203) 226-6967

Metatec/Discovery Systems
7001 Discovery Boulevard.
Dublin, OH 43017
(614) 761-2000

Microsoft Corporation
One Microsoft Way
Redmond, WA 98052
(206) 882-8080

National Geographic Society
17th and M Streets, NW
Washington, DC 20036
(202) 857-7378

New Media Schoolhouse
390 Westchester Avenue.
Pound Ridge, NY 10576
(800) 672-6002

Origin Systems, Inc.
12940 Research
Austin, TX 78750
(512) 328-5490

Peter J. Phethean Ltd.
1640 E. Brookdale Avenue.
La Habra, CA 90631
(714) 990-5524

Quanta Press, Inc.
1313 Fifth Street, Suite 208C
Minneapolis, MN 55414
(612) 379-3956

Starware Publishing Corp.
P.O. Box 4188
Deerfield Beach, FL 33442
(305) 426-4552

Tiger Media
5801 East Slauson Avenue, Suite 200
Los Angeles, CA 90040
(213) 721-8282

UniDisc, Inc.
3941 Cherryvale Avenue., Suite 1
Soquel, CA 95073
(408) 464-0707

Warner New Media
3500 Olive Avenue.
Burbank, CA 91505
(818) 955-9999

Wolfetone Multimedia Publishing Company
1010 Huntcliff, Suite 1350
Atlanta, GA 30350
(404) 992-7500

World Library, Inc.
12914 Haster Street
Garden Grove, CA 92640
(714) 748-7197

Xiphias
8758 Venice Boulevard
Los Angeles, CA 90034
(310) 841-2790

ACCESSORIES, COMPONENTS, SYSTEMS, MASTERING/REPLICATION

General Technics
38 Raynor Avenue
Ronkonkoma, NY 11779
(800) 487-2538
(computers, cases, cables, drives, and so forth)

QB Products
1260 Karl Court
Wauconda, IL 60084
(800) 323-6856
(caddies and CD storage units)

Nimbus Information Systems
P.O. Box 7305
Charlottesville, VA 22906
(804) 985-1100
(CD-ROM mastering, one-offs, replication, and publishing)

Recoton Corporation/Discwasher
46-23 Crane Street
Long Island City, NY 11101
(718) 392-6009
(CD cleaners, storage units, and accessories)

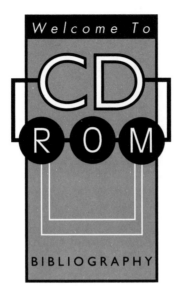

PRINT MEDIA

Graf, Rudolf F. *Modern Dictionary of Electronics.* Howard W. Sams & Sons Co., 1977.

Woodcock, Joanne, et al. *Computer Dictionary.* Microsoft Press, 1991.

Toffler, Alvin. *The Third Wave.* William Morrow and Co., Inc., 1980.

Software Publishers Association. *Compact Disc Special Interest Group Resource Guide.* Disc Manufacturing, Inc., 1992.

Benford, Tom. *"Installing a CD-ROM Drive." ComputerCraft Magazine,* August 1992.

OPTICAL MEDIA

Microsoft Multimedia Bookshelf. (CD-ROM—1992 Edition), Microsoft Corporation.

CD-ROM Sampler. (CD-ROM), Metatec/Discovery Systems.

The CD-ROM Directory, 1992. (7th & 8th CD-ROM Editions), UniDisc, Inc.

CD-ROMS in Print—1992. (CD-ROM edition), Meckler Corporation.

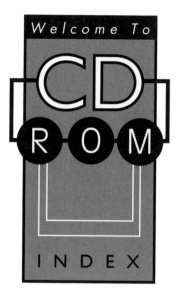

Welcome To CD ROM

INDEX

"So what is a Multimedia Magazine on CD ROM, anyway?"

Imagine a magazine that would not only tell you about new software but let you experience it. Not only tell you about a new song but let you listen to it. Not only tell you about a new game but let you challenge it. Not only tell you about new shareware but let you install it and explore the benefits firsthand.

Seeing *and hearing* is believing. That's why we're not going to leave it up to your imagination. We want to send you **two CD ROMs** for a very special *Welcome to... CD ROM* price: First we'll send you an **Introduction to Nautilus** CD ROM so you can see and hear what a multimedia magazine can be. Then one month later we'll send you the **current issue of Nautilus** and you'll see why thousands of subscribers worldwide rely on Nautilus to keep them informed and entertained every month.

Both Nautilus CD ROMs can be yours for only $9.95 shipping and handling (VISA/MasterCard accepted). Call 800/637-3472 today to begin your two-disc Nautilus experience. (International callers: 614/766-3165.)

Receive two discs and experience the next generation in magazines...

Nautilus℠

METATEC
Corporation

Macintosh Requirements: Mac® Plus or higher, 2.5 MB RAM, System 6.0.5 or higher, CD ROM drive.
Windows Requirements: IBM® or compatible with Windows 3.0 (with Multimedia extensions) or higher, CD ROM drive.
Nautilus • 7001 Discovery Boulevard, Dublin, Ohio 43017-3299
Nautilus is a servicemark of Metatec Corporation.
All others are copyright of their respective owners.
Prices subject to change.

Multimedia
presentations and information on the latest tools and how to use them

Entertainment
games, contests, music and more for hours of fun

Sounds
music and sound effects digitized and ready to use, *plus* MIDI files to hear and play

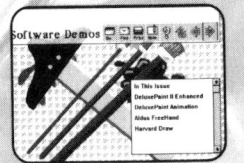

Software
demos and reviews of popular programs, plus shareware and "free use" software